Experiencing Sacredness: A Psycho-Spiritu

Table of Contents

Dedication

To All Those Seekers of Redemption

Foreword

John Moritsugu

I vividly remember the first time I met Lenny Jason. We were incoming graduate students at the University of Rochester. At orientation, a thin, long-haired fellow wearing jeans and wire-rimmed glasses made his way toward the back and sat down next to me. Giving in to my stereotypes and the times, I thought to myself, "a hippy."

I had many questions about him. I would soon have most of those questions answered as we were classmates in the same program and over time, good friends. That friendship has lasted for over 50 years. And yet, there were many things I discovered in his newest book.

In "Experiencing Sacredness: A Psycho-Spiritual journey," Lenny shares the part of his life's journey that brought him to the University of Rochester on that bright Fall day in 1971. Through a series of stories, we learn of his private pilgrimage undertaken in search of life's truths in the summer before he began his graduate training in psychology. For those who know Lenny and his work, it is not surprising that this journey was undertaken with the dedication of an ascetic. These revelatory stories show us his development and maturation through his interactions with people and his confrontations with the challenges of travel.

Over the years, those in psychology have come to know Lenny as a tireless researcher who has taken on a wide range of topics. He and his students have worked on definitions of community psychology, and the varieties of a "psychological sense of community", as well as many practical and applied topics. More recently, his research and writing have examined Oxford House (a self-run, self-sustaining, recovery home program), helped to define and understand chronic fatigue syndrome (myalgic encephalomyelitis), and studied the effects of long term COVID. His voluminous body of work has earned Lenny national recognition and awards.

For those who would like to know more about Lenny, the book contains stories and reflections on his search for the sacred in life and how to attain it. From London to India and back, with significant stops along the way, we journey with him on this quest. We come to appreciate his underlying empathy and compassion, and the patterns which have contributed to his prodigious achievements. Experiencing sacredness captures Lenny Jason and the subtext of his work.

Preface

———

As a newly minted graduate from Brandeis University, I was eager to begin my trip to India. Maybe graduate school and psychology would be in the cards, or possibly a life path not yet conceived, but now I needed knowledge via adventure.

With long-held interests in Eastern religions and philosophy, I thought trading what I had only read in library books for real-world experiences would offer a different compass to find a life of happiness and fulfillment. With some trusty cash in my wallet and 500 bucks in traveler's checks, along with surely folded maps of Europe and the Middle East, I was set to begin my voyage to India.

To many people who knew about my plans, it was just another hippie's summer road trip. After all, taking a few months off and backpacking through Europe or Asia was far from unique, and while my location was slightly unorthodox, my goals were not. You could call it whatever you like—a journey to sacredness, a spiritual awakening, a coming-of-age tale, or simply finding myself.

In a way, it was all of those things. I was looking for something. I wouldn't be able to define what exactly until I had found it, and I knew I might never be able to accurately describe it to anyone. That might sound pretentious, in the way that traveling with nothing but a backpack and traveler's checks could, but I stood at the precipice of the next stage of my life. I was without a clear idea as to what might bring me fulfillment or who I wanted to become. All I knew was that the answer didn't lie behind a desk, in a book, or even with an academic degree.

EXPERIENCING SACREDNESS: A PSYCHO-SPIRITUAL JOURNEY

I hoped it could be found while trekking through vast deserts and lands shrouded in mystery, sitting with strangers at a roadside café, or even during quiet moments of panic when I found myself in previously unimaginable peril. The glorious mystery of life lived in the blurry spaces where the line between inspiration and tragedy ceased to exist or was tenuous at best and where complete strangers became confidants.

My journey to find sacredness was as unique and varied as how all such adventurers begin and end. My hope is that as you turn these pages and thus step into my shoes and meet those who enlightened me, you may start to find the same intangible things that led me halfway around the world and returned me as a different person.

Lenny Jason

LENNY JASON

6

My Brandeis Graduation Yearbook Photo

Chapter 1: Rites of Passage

―――

Prior Adventures

Why the heck did I think I'd be a modern-day Christ overlanding through Europe and the Middle East to reach India, in my youthful quest for self-illumination? I figured this journey through 14 countries would be a piece of cake as I had previously traveled to France and hitchhiked around the U.S. But those prior adventures only established a risky state of overconfidence.

One of these adventures occurred after my sophomore year of college. I had flown to Paris to take an introductory French course at the Alliance Française and had then summoned the audacity to enroll in a history course at the Sorbonne. The registrar asked if I was comfortable speaking French, and of course, I used my two favorite words: oui oui.

That silly boast about my abilities got me in. Fortunately, my history professor spoke French slowly enough for me to understand most of his arcane lectures. Still, later each night, I read relevant historical books in English to be sure I understood the material.

I chuckled as he profusely sprayed spit as he lectured. It took only one time of being the direct repository for me to stay clear of the front rows.

I had to shift my weight throughout the lectures as I sat on the stiff wooden benches. The atmosphere was stuffy, pretentious, and formal. Only paid attendants were allowed to raise or lower the ancient, dark window blinds in the austere classrooms.

Still, I was blessed to be studying in one of the first universities in the world, founded in 1253 by Robert de Sorbon, a King's chaplain. When it got stuffy and hot in the classroom, I imagined myself as a knight in medieval Europe, surrounded by classical architecture.

I loved Paris' wide boulevards and spectacular landmarks, including the Eiffel Tower and Notre Dame Cathedral, the ubiquitous outdoor cafes, and the Metro subway system that delivered me to the Latin Quarter.

I was fortunate to live with a delightful French farming family about six miles from Paris in Choisy-le-Roi, where we ate sumptuous dinners and talked into the night about scandalous village intrigue.

I enjoyed playing with the friendly, free-roaming rabbits on their farm. One cream-colored rabbit with two brown spots on its back was particularly friendly. I named her Cookie. She would spot me walking over and rush to greet me. I'd lift her and coddle her up to my chest like she was a kitten. She was fluffy and warm but, unlike cats, didn't purr. Still, it was fun to caress her fur, and it made me feel welcome in a faraway land.

One day, twilight descending, I walked to the rabbit pen, but Cookie didn't hop to greet me. The pen was empty of the eight rabbits that lived there. Confused, I walked back to the house where I came upon Morris, my host.

"Where are the rabbits?" I asked. "Did they run off?"

Morris had a hearty laugh soaked with nicotine. "No, no," he said and motioned me to follow him.

We walked into the back of the large pantry, where a boxy fridge stood in the far corner. Morris raised the cover, smiled with pride, and then rubbed his opulent belly.

Rabbit Image released CC0

"Now we eat."

I peeked in and saw the skinned bodies of eight rabbits. I couldn't tell which one was Cookie's. I felt the tears rise in my throat but swallowed quickly, pushing away what I thought Morris would find childish behavior. I'd by then been a devout vegetarian for several years. I found the thought of eating an animal morbid and cruel. I also understood that Morris wasn't a bad person. He just preferred a meat diet. I've met many kind people who love meat. I've also met vegetarians who were jerks.

Another time, I was thrilled to see a flock of migrating ducks that landed on the property's pond. Later that day, over lunch, I asked Morris. "I see you have visiting ducks in your pond. Will they be staying on?"

My host grinned and rubbed his stomach. He went into the kitchen closet and returned with a large net. "Do you wish to help with supper?"

Once again dismayed, I pretended to eye my watch.

"Uh, no...but thanks. I have to...uh...meet some friends," and left before I could be enlisted into the fowl assassination team.

One evening in Paris, I unexpectedly encountered my friend Jim from Brandeis. I hadn't heard that Jim would be traveling through France. Weed might have been his best friend, as he often stood for hours next to a Brandeis building with a stoned, mischievous smile on his face. That meeting in Paris was the evening that Neil Armstrong landed on the moon, which was televised late at night from an appliance store that had TV screens on display. Jim was convinced that he'd traveled to the moon many times during his altered states of consciousness, so as far as he was concerned, Armstrong wasn't the first to step on that large pumpkin in the sky.

It was late, and I'd missed the last train back to Choisy-le-Roi, so I slept on the uncomfortable wooden floor in Jim's rented room in a poor part of Paris. I was woken up in the early morning by the balding and overweight hotel manager who was maniacally pounding on my head while screaming in French, "Get out! Get out! You cannot sleep here!"

I scrambled to get out of the room.

When my coursework was finished, I decided to travel to Sweden. I was lucky to catch a ride with one of my professors and one of his friends but was packed into the back of his white Peugeot with all the luggage, just like a sardine in a roll-top can. I stuck my head out the window like a panting dog since I wanted to experience the crisp, fresh air of the spectacular old-growth German forests.

In Sweden, I could strip down in a sauna, sweat, and then jump into a freezing lake. Colors became brighter, and life seemed full of new possibilities.

I came across a spa in Sweden that had a large sauna perched on the shores of a lake with close-to-freezing water. I decided to 'be a Roman in Rome' and try out the local customs. The sauna was hotter than I expected, but I stayed in it for 30 minutes. I was surrounded by a dozen serious-looking and crusty older men who seemed perfectly comfortable staying in the sauna forever, perhaps even spending the night and ordering food delivery.

My skin sizzling, I walked out to the deck leading to the lake and came upon an elderly woman who smiled at me and carried on in Swedish.

"I'm sorry," I said in English, "but I don't speak Swedish."

"You American?"

"Yes, madam, just passing through."

"And you going to swim in this cold water?" she asked and pointed to the placid lake.

"I was planning on that," and stuck my toe in the water, "but I might change my mind."

"You Americans can be loud and rude," the lady said without a trace of condescension in her remark like she was simply stating a fact known to all.

I'd encountered the Ugly American phenomenon and found it to be true at times. "Yeah, some of us can get pretty obnoxious."

She chuckled. "I do not believe you swim in this lake. It too cold for an American."

Now that was a challenge that I decided to face. "Really? Well, I got news for you, lady. Watch this."

I rushed to the water and dove into the icy abyss; my skin was still red and sweaty from the sauna. My lungs seized up while my skin tingled with a million needles.

The elderly lady walked into the lake and submerged in it like she was taking a warm bath. Then she took off swimming in measured strokes while I stayed close to shore. My teeth chattered like a busy typewriter.

I rushed back to shore and back to the sauna. It was an invigorating experience but once was enough.

The next week I spent traveling through Sweden, Norway, and Denmark.

I finished the summer by attending the electric, jubilant atmosphere of the Isle of Wight British festival, which featured Bob Dylan and The Band, The Who, and Joe Cocker. The highlight was when Dylan, who had been in semi-retirement for a few years, arrived on stage in a cream suit.

Woodstock holds the torch for the hippie revolution in the '60s, but the Isle of White was better. The weather was perfect, so we weren't engulfed in frosty rain and pools of mud like in Woodstock. The sound system was great, and the Who rocked hard, leaving a stage littered with eviscerated guitars and drums. The crowd was mellow as can be, and everyone (except me) was stoned or tripping on acid. Many girls danced topless in celebration of women's lib, and the lads were cordial and supportive in mannered ways.

I was about 100 feet from the stage when Dylan came on. People were packed on one another, but we all swayed in mellow vibes. The guy next to me, a tall Scandinavian with long blonde hair in a ponytail, turned to me and said, "You want to fly?"

"Fly? I'm not sure what you mean?"

He opened his palm and showed me the acid dot. "You want to fly?"

I grinned. I loved the vibe but wasn't attracted to psychedelics, which I suspected could be fun but could also take you where you've never been before and from where you ain't coming back.

"I'm okay, but don't mind me. Go ahead and fly as high as you wish."

"I will," and he licked the dot off his palm.

Dylan's nasally voice is marginal, and his harmonica playing is adequate at best, but none of that mattered when he delivered his surreal, honest messages in songs such as "Like a Rolling Stone." The Band backed him up and took his music to the next level. The tall Scandinavian was soon cruising when he looked at me with wide eyes and dilated pupils. "I'm flying now."

"You are indeed," I said and almost felt a contact buzz.

During these travels, I had no concerns that any harm would come to me.

Hitching Across the US

The experience most relevant to the one I was about to embark on occurred after my junior year at Brandeis University. I was inspired by Steinbeck's cross-country trip across the U.S., and just like that, I set out to hitchhike across the country and started by heading down to New Orleans.

New Orleans is a different world from the Northeast. It has a thick, warm buzz in the air that oozes over its residents and slows them down. There is good food, plenty of drink, and a dark underside that always lurks nearby. It was the opposite of the cold weather and fast-paced lifestyle of the Northeasterners.

And now began my most memorable early encounter. I met Twinkie in the French Quarter, the first transvestite I had ever met. He was minuscule, barely five feet tall, and one hundred pounds soaking wet. Tiny but mighty, as I soon learned. Wearing bright red clothes, Twinkie walked to be noticed and noticed he was. Whistles and romantic offers were met by Twinkie's confident smile and head tilt. Not one passerby made a nasty offer. Twinkie had a take-no-shit aura, and the guys could see it.

Lucky for me, Twinkie took an interest in me. He was a kind and non-judgmental person. He was proud to play his self-appointed role as ambassador of New Orleans and show me the sights, including those the tourists never see. We ate fried dough covered in powdered sugar, called beignets. Twinkie only ate a few and gave me the rest. I guess he was watching his figure. I wolfed down mine and his. They sat in my stomach like a brick.

Twinkie must have known that because he led me through the back door of an out-of-the-way jazz club and ordered a ginger ale for me. It was a small, dark, smoky place with amazing jazz musicians who were wildly jamming in all sorts of bizarre keys.

One local, inebriated and confused by the dark and his blurry vision, ambled over and asked Twinkie if he could buy him a drink.

"Can I join you and your boyfriend? Some wine per..."

The local suddenly reacquired his eyesight, gulped in embarrassment, and stumbled out of the club, muttering strangled curses.

Twinkie grinned and patted my hand. "Don't worry, honey. I'll take that as a compliment."

The nearby patrons laughed and toasted Twinkie with raised glasses.

There are few places for jazz, like New Orleans. I didn't see one tourist in that club, just locals enjoying the groove of the music and the kick in their drinks. I told Twinkie the ginger ale had melted the "beignets brick" in my stomach.

"You're welcome, honey," he said in his raspy voice.

We said our goodbyes after a few sets of music. Twinkie made me promise to look him up if I ever passed through his city again.

The next day, I thought I'd check out a New Orleans beach before I headed to Houston, Texas. It was strange to see a segregated beach in 1970; I hadn't seen that sort of thing in the Northeast. But instead of a beautiful beach, I soon saw angry white locals screaming and chasing four African-American boys who came too close to their area. I quickly left the beach and stuck my thumb out as soon as I was on the main road. I hitched to Houston with no problems. Or so I imagined.

Years later, I learned that a serial killer, Dean Corll, had tortured and murdered at least 28 teenage boys and young men between 1970—1973 in the same Houston area where I was obliviously hitching rides. My success in hitching was built on false confidence, as I was unaware of the dark side that exists in people. I later realized how lucky I'd been when I finally learned the gruesome details of the murders.

As I headed north, I spotted an advertisement on the highway that was hiring drivers. I got hired to transport two enormous separate but connected trucks from Arizona to Southern California, even though I had never driven a truck. The representative at the truck company showed me how to work the clutches, and off I went.

There I was, six feet above the freeway and driving the massive vehicle. The sophomoric joy of at once feeling childish wonder while feeling 'like a man' was lots of fun. I felt the power of the engine seep into my bones and sensed the 'open road' sensation glamorized in movies.

An 18-wheeler zipped by and honked its brass horn. I gave the driver a thumbs up, but he'd already disappeared. Another 18-wheeler zipped by, and another one after that, and both honked their horns. I wondered if the honking involved some ritual of welcoming the rookie into the fold, so when the next truck was about to pass me, I rolled down the window, stuck out my arm, and gave the honking driver a thumbs up. He, in turn, gave me the finger.

My Drivers's License

I sat deflated and wondered what was happening when I noticed the speedometer. I was driving 35 mph and quickly gathered they were honking cause I was being a nuisance and not fitting in with the traffic flow. I slowly increased the pressure on the gas pedal until I was cruising at 55 mph, and when the honking stopped.

Now, whenever I see these rigs on the road, I cringe and hope the operators have more driver training preparation than I did.

EXPERIENCING SACREDNESS: A PSYCHO-SPIRITUAL JOURNEY

Following that irresponsible venture, I was hitchhiking when I got picked up by a bunch of hippies who were headed to Mexico to buy gold with stolen credit cards. These hustlers thought of themselves as regular capitalists, just businesspeople doing their bit to make a living. I was intrigued by this mafia-inspired group but politely refused their offer to be initiated into their clan to become "made." We parted ways after a few days.

Another time, I got picked up by a driver who looked quite ordinary. He was dressed in a neat, formal suit and tie; everything in his car was in meticulous order.

An hour into the drive, he asked, "Are you into whips and chains?"

"Excuse me?"

"You know, whips and chains. You can tie me up if you prefer. I dig it."

"Excuse me?"

He chuckled. "Don't worry, it's fun, and we always have a safe word?"

"Safe word?"

"Yeah, so no one feels threatened."

"I'm sorry, sir, but I have no idea what you mean."

"I'm sorry," he said, a genuine inflection in his voice. "I didn't mean to freak you out. I'm no serial killer or something."

"Oh...okay," I mumbled through my sandpaper-dry throat and decided it was time to say goodbye to this odd dude. "Can we stop for a minute? I need to pee."

"Sure," said the whips and chains hobbyist.

Shortly after, we pulled into a gas station, and I said, "Thanks for the ride."

He shrugged. "Okay, safe travels."

I waited till he drove off and then headed back to the road and stuck out my thumb. My rushing heart took a while to wind down.

That summer, I meandered through about 40 states, encountering dozens of people who positively and warmly welcomed me into their lives. I occasionally walked into unguarded train yards, where I found empty railroad cars and hobos. My fellow freeloaders were a motley group. One pretended to be a chicken with his head cut off and made clucking noises for our amusement. Another one, nicknamed "Carpenter Joe," had lost his family in a car accident. His forlorn stare clearly stated his abandonment of society. They had all encountered lousy luck, had fallen on hard times, and were just trying to survive long enough to find their next meal and destination.

I also spent time working in a State Mental Hospital in Pueblo, Colorado. I realized that the psychiatric patients were saner than many of the supposedly sane folk I'd met while hitchhiking. Most of these troubled souls were good people whose worlds had collapsed for a variety of reasons. I was fascinated by their stories of pain and disappointment. One patient had been raped by her father, another was dealing with out-of-control alcohol addiction, and still, another had psychotic visions of being some type of god.

One patient who was waif-like, with long red hair, stood next to me while I was filling out forms. She held a comic book as she flirted with me.

"You're cute. I'm Jemma. Do you like me?'

I wasn't sure what to say. We had been instructed to avoid personal relationships with the patients.

She grinned at me, then seductively flipped her hair.

The next thing I knew, she was behind me, and I felt pressure on the back of my neck. I wondered if it might be a knife, but I remained calm and kept talking. It turned out it was her finger that was touching my neck. She giggled maniacally, kissed me on my forehead, and pranced down the hallway, singing way off-pitch.

The professional staff were distant and not meaningfully connected to the patients, which reminded me of Ken Kesey's description of a mental hospital in *One Flew Over the Cuckoo's Nest*.

There were many similarities between the hobos and the people with mental health conditions, as many Americans are just one paycheck away from being homeless - and homeless people can end up as hobos, or even wind up in a mental hospital. They can be normal people who are just down on their luck, suffering from the loss of a job or a personal tragedy that has sent them into a depression, or into the terrible spiral of drug or alcohol addiction.

I'd never felt threatened or in any real danger during these two summer trips. I figured if I could spend a summer in Paris and hitch around the U.S., it would be no problem hitchhiking to India. I had no idea that my structured summer in Paris or my travels in the U.S. would be nothing like what I'd experienced in the Middle East and India.

A Conversation with Friends

Image from Mike Lovett by en.wikipedia

Before my trip to India and a few days before graduating from Brandeis University in June 1971, I walked past an old castle, which now housed Cholmondeley's coffeehouse and Brandeis student dorms. As I passed the Usdan Student Center, I met two old Brandeis friends, Allen and Roger, who joined me as we walked through the spacious, green quad in the back of the University library. We sat in the shade in front of a heart-shaped pool next to the Jewish synagogue and the Catholic and Protestant chapels, which presented a message of interreligious cooperation.

The pastoral setting was misleading. The air was packed with tension. It seemed the U.S. was coming apart at the seams. The young people walking the campus trails were embroiled in confusion, anger, and questioning everything that was fed to them while growing up. The body bags were coming back from Vietnam. Everyone knew someone who'd been drafted, and many knew someone who never made it back or did with an arm or a leg missing. The quest to fight 'the man' and take down 'the system' was alive in many young hearts. Many years later, it's fair to say that the revolution we quested succeeded with mixed results.

Roger, a tall, slender, studious-looking undergrad, said, "Jason, congrats on finishing up. Good to see you outta the library for a change."

"I will miss staying till closing every night. At least it kept me out of trouble," I replied.

Roger smiled, "Still a wise guy. Hey, heard you're going off to India after graduation. That's something."

"Yeah, I need to answer some questions. I'm gonna hitchhike from London and then through Europe and the Middle East."

Allen, a thin and gregarious undergrad, blurted out, "Ya gotta be kidding."

Sprouting a red beard, Allen was the kind of guy who would keep quiet until he finally focused on something he considered important.

"Why are you yearning to go to India and not China, Egypt, or the other sacred hot spots? Are you having flashes of déjà vu about your past life as an Indian holy man?"

"Very funny," I said, miffed at his irreverence.

"Going with anyone?" Roger asked.

I shook my head. "Nope, going alone."

Roger's eyes widened. "Parents okay with this?"

"I mentioned it to them," I said. "Mom was a bit worried, but Dad didn't have much to say. They pretty much let me do what I want. Always been that way."

"Man, that's not the way with my family." Roger shook his head and looked wistful and distant.

"Makes sense you'd go there, I guess. You've always been interested in the East and mysticism. Remember the sociology class we took with Professor Morrie Schwartz? It was more like an encounter group, with all of us sitting on the floor in a circle."

I nodded. "I remember it. We all had to give feedback on how we came across."

Roger sighed, "What a course. I never forgot the initial 15 minutes of our first class. We all sat there looking at each other, trying not to stare, trying not to look away, trying to figure out who would break the silence. That class helped me gain some insights about how I was perceived by others. I still see Morrie around campus prancing around like a madman. What a free spirit."

I added, "He's one of my favorite professors. That class was like a group therapy session. We shared all types of personal things, like the time that guy told us that he lost his virginity just the night before."

Roger retorted, "That was you, Jason."

"Who, me?" I could barely contain my mischievous smile as I continued.

"I felt comfortable telling that class anything. I also loved meeting Abraham Maslow. He helped me see the world in a new way."

EXPERIENCING SACREDNESS: A PSYCHO-SPIRITUAL JOURNEY

Morrie Schwartz's life was later popularized in the book, *Tuesdays with Morrie*. Maslow's work on Self-Actualization and the hierarchy of needs helped found the influential Humanistic Psychology movement. These and other teachers who influenced me at Brandeis are described in Appendix A as well as more political issues regarding Angela Davis, Abbie Hoffman, Susan Saxe, and the massacre at Kent State that we discussed during this conversation.

Then Allen said, "So this upcoming trip, hitchhiking through those countries, so cool."

"Yep, I'm looking forward to it. Just staying open to any experience that comes my way. I hope to meet some holy men and see what I can learn."

We looked at each other with a strange mixture of joy and fear of the unknown future.

I shrugged. "Who knows? Maybe I'll stay there and enter some type of ashram."

Roger raised his brow. "What if you get into trouble? What'll you do then?"

"No idea, but I hope I can handle it on my own. I'm only bringing about 500 bucks in traveler's checks, so if I lose them, I can get my money back. Guess that's some protection."

Allen was not convinced. "So much shit's happening in this country. You should stay and get involved in our political struggles."

I shook my head. "Lots of things have to change, but I need to take this trip now. Maybe then I'll be better at whatever I decide to do with my life. So much is bubbling up in me now, and I'm trying to make sense of it."

"I've read so many books and had many great conversations. Now I need to experience the world, as I have not done before. I'll be on my own, traveling in lands I know very little about, with an openness to finding my teachers from wherever they might come."

Roger nodded. "Makes sense to me. And whatever you learn from your trip, be sure to let us know. You're headed for either India, some sort of enlightenment, or graduate school. Kind of like a fork in the road, and whatever path you take will be right. I'm sure of that."

Allen rubbed his chin and nodded. "I know; I can't wait to see the book you write on this. So here's the sales pitch for the book. I have a winning story to tell in this memoir, and with more and more of our generation clueless about what they want to do with their lives, they'll be absorbed and delighted to hear of my overland rite of passage to India. Americans are looking for the inspiration they will get in my travel story, and the timing for my book is great, as there is a pent-up demand for an adventure due to the civil unrest in this country."

Laughing at this proposal, I said, "Sure, you can help me shape and transform my overly anal and pedantic writing style so that we can give the world an engaging, riveting, and spellbinding masterpiece."

Allen agreed. "We'll make lots of money with a best seller."

I chuckled. "I don't think so. I'm just a left-brained-oriented voyager who would write a sophomoric rite of passage memoir, and it would need to have a creative right-brained writer to exorcise it of my dry writing style."

Laughing at this comedy, Roger added his thoughts. "No way. You're gonna give Kerouac a run for his money."

I ended the conversation by saying, "Don't bet on it. Roger, and Allen, you guys are true friends. I'll never forget you."

EXPERIENCING SACREDNESS: A PSYCHO-SPIRITUAL JOURNEY

My Trip Begins

In the summer of 1971, I embarked on an overland trip to India via Europe, Turkey, Iran, Afghanistan, and Pakistan. I was alone and the journey proved more than a bit perilous. I survived the dangers that presented themselves, and in the end, as I revisited the many experiences along the way, I realized it was much more than a road trip through India. It was the adventure of a lifetime.

Some may consider my travels to have been foolish, even reckless, but similar adjectives could be applied to all personal rites of passage. Indeed, I was searching to find a true purpose for my life and had entered an extremely dark and dense forest through which I was utterly determined to penetrate and navigate alone.

I'd have had it no other way. I would encounter many unforeseen challenges along with breathtaking, exhilarating moments and images, all of which provided new insights into what might bring me happiness, fulfillment, and an appreciation of the sacred. Any success in life—including a profound understanding of what is truly sacred—requires a great deal of boldness.

The Eastern religions I'd read about had become increasingly appealing to me. They hinted at a way of approaching life with a certain reverence for the here and now, regardless of the circumstances. Buddhism spoke about releasing us from the enchantment of Maya, or illusion. By breaking through the limitations of ego, we might behold a paradise where one has a sense of compassion and empathy for the terror and suffering that are part of this world and where one might be free to experience the awe and mystery of the universe.

Was I searching for these new ways of being in the world? My culture and religion had urged me to defeat the forces of darkness and seek refuge in the light. Good and evil existed, and I was told that our job was to battle the evil forces. Still, eastern philosophies spoke about a reality where both good and evil might be part of our very nature and that coming to grips with this fundamental paradox might be one of life's greatest mysteries. Perhaps my quest in traveling to the Far East was to explore this different kind of reality.

These were the questions I had as I began my journey. I'd soon make my way to Iran and Afghanistan and later to India and other exotic locations. I encountered thieves, beggars, con men, holy men, and all types of kindness and charity from the world's poorest yet most noble inhabitants.

I was a wet-behind-the-ears student with an interest in Maslow and compassionate psychology. I wanted to explore Eastern religion at the source and maybe, just maybe, find a way to reconcile my emotional life with the possibility of redemption through a broader understanding of the world. And that...I would do. Please join me and see the wonders of my journey through your imagination. Let's go!

Chapter 2: On the Road to India

First Stop England

While in the air, far above the expansive Atlantic, I reflected on my upcoming voyage to India. I needed to uncover who I had become over 22 years. I was, to some extent, a mystery to myself and was desperate to discern which of my qualities to keep and which to shed—like clothing, which suited its time but now clearly worn threadbare. I would let unravel past ways of perceiving the world.

I didn't bring a camera. I wanted my memory to store the insights of my trip without the trappings of photos—it can give you the colors, but only your mind gives you the feeling. My trip would not be some posh vacation in gleaming, towering five-star hotels. I would live close to the land; I'd hitchhike for transportation. If I found myself strapped for cash, part-time work would offer more lessons for much-needed growth. I had no schedule, no pre-ordained path, just staying flexible so I could be an explorer with each new day filled with adventures. I hoped to learn from locals about the ways of their culture if they were kind enough to share them.

I thought of spiritual journeys described in worn, yellowed paperbacks I used to purchase with loose change. I was hoping there would be lessons to learn from a different way of experiencing the world—one more balanced and in harmony with the world.

W. Somerset Maugham's *The Razor's Edge* sprang into my consciousness, where Larry Darrell finds his bohemian life in Paris meaningless and gives up security and personal relationships to seek spiritual meaning in his life. Other heroes and anti-heroes passed before my eyes. Where would I fall on the spectrum?

I recalled wandering around Harvard Square one chilly spring afternoon when I came upon a group of Hare Krishna devotees dancing to the beat of tambourines and bongos. Their worship of foreign gods clashed with my Western independence and autonomy, but they seemed happy. A blonde woman about my age came up to me and held my hand. "Come join us."

Her hand was soft and warm. I smiled nervously. "You don't wanna see me dance; I'm all elbows and knees."

She laughed. "Who cares? Krishna loves you no matter how you dance."

Her blue eyes shone with happiness, and I could smell her lavender hair. The fleeting thought crossed my mind that I could fall in love with her, that somehow my romantic yearnings could be met by joining her on the journey to Krishna's Bliss. My brain intervened and clouded my heart's romance.

I pulled my hand away. "I appreciate your quest, but I'm not ready."

"Okay," she said and returned to the dancing circle. I walked off with the quiet intent to learn more about spiritual practices that might open this new world to me.

I considered the Chinese philosophical ideas of Lao Tsu, which presented a different way of experiencing the world in the *Tao Te Ching*, where a wise person could work and take in their surroundings without effort. I shouldn't try too hard, I told myself. You can't collect experiences like bent baseball cards flapping in the spokes; you sometimes have to let them in, no matter how intimidating.

It was always easy for me to be good in school, but now my education would occur on the roads, in homes, and in villages in the countries I'd soon visit.

EXPERIENCING SACREDNESS: A PSYCHO-SPIRITUAL JOURNEY

As I felt the plane's sharp descent into London, the first leg of the journey now becoming real, I felt a song humming lightly from within: "You know it don't come easy"— Ringo Starr may not have been known as the most enlightened Beatle, but his words still ring true — the song hinted at possibly deeper perhaps unconscious understandings of what might occur over the upcoming months.

Passport Photo

And then I landed. In their methodological, efficient fashion, the British enabled travelers to leave the airport and arrive in London in one hour.

London was an adventure, each new sight unique, quaint, and fascinating. Its history started in 50 A.D. when it was a Roman settlement and later became the Capital city of the Roman Empire's Northern Province. There are hundreds of breathtaking old and contemporary buildings with architectural styles from Baroque, Georgian, Regency, Victorian, and Edwardian. It was exciting to be in this Capital, which has been on the world stage for centuries.

Encounters with a Bank Guard

After arriving in London, I visited a bank to purchase their local currency. The building conveyed a sense of dual stability and strength for its customers, with its classic architecture and solid construction.

I noticed a guard standing near the entrance. As I walked past him, he smiled as he did to other customers. The guard was of medium height and donned a police uniform, yet he maintained an aura of encouragement in place of roughness.

I stood by a counter and watched him greet one customer after another; he held a friendly, broad, and warm smile. He seemed content with his job, and I wondered how he created his reality in a job that seemed so ordinary.

Image by A P Monblat from CC BY-SA 3.0

EXPERIENCING SACREDNESS: A PSYCHO-SPIRITUAL JOURNEY

I thought he was a hero, just as in Camus's Myth of Sisyphus. Every time Sisyphus pushed a stone up a hill, it would roll back down, and then he would have to push it up again. Many would think of the bank guard's job as rather dull, with the same routine every day. However, I believed like Sisyphus; he challenged the universe by infusing meaning into it. I didn't have a conversation with him, or see the bank guard talking to others; I just observed him. His presence was striking as he reached out in a subtle way to every person who passed him. He would catch their eyes as if he'd known them for a long time.

I realized I could learn as much from observing valuable transactions as from having conversations. I had been taught that it was through "words" that we understand the themes in literature, philosophy, and life. Western education stressed cognitive ways of knowing but I could gain insights and wisdom from just watching what was in front of me. I realized that feelings and emotions that emerge from observing simple nonverbal behaviors could transmit important meaning about people, their circumstances, and their ways of being in the world.

In my brief observation of the bank teller, I learned a valuable lesson: anyone can greet the day by smiling at others and making a difference in the smallest way. It was the first spiritual lesson on my trip. I could tear down the boundaries of ordinary existence that often involved thinking of the past or future, and that in each moment, there is a spectacular alternative way of being alive in the world, and that way of being in the world was always in front of me.

I wondered what kept me from smiling at others or greeting others with "Hello, how is your day going?" or "That is a nice outfit you have on." It would not matter what was said to others. The positive greeting would be a way of welcoming the ordinary walk with openness and vitality that could be shared with others.

31

As I left the bank, I gave it a try and started smiling as I walked past people; sure enough, many smiled back. After smiling at an elderly woman, she said, "Hello. How is your day?"

"Good, actually pretty amazing. How's your day?"

"It's good but probably not as good as yours. You look happy."

"I am."

Then she smiled. The deep wrinkles on her forehead and cheeks seemed to recede and let through her younger self from many years ago.

I pledged to be friendly to others I'd meet at parks and coffee houses, which would help me get to know the locals and their customs. Being receptive to seeing the extraordinary in every moment was the spiritual gift the bank guard had given me.

The British: Proud and Reserved

Wandering the streets of London brought me to stand by a pub called The Boar's Head. I ventured in. It had a musty scent like most pubs in London but not entirely unpleasant. Surely enough, a boar's head was mounted over the bar. Its red beady eyes glittered, and its tasks were long and sharp.

I saddled up at the bar and tried to do as the English do: order a Guinness Stout. I took a sip and puckered my lips, realizing that drinking warm, bitter beer is an acquired taste.

The fellow sitting next to me looked up and said, "What's wrong? Beer taste bad?"

"I'm not sure," I replied.

Hearing my accent, he said, "Well, your American beer isn't exactly known for quality."

"Can't argue that," I said, "so I might keep practicing."

The man chuckled and took a long swig from his mug. "What's up with you Yanks anyway, getting into that war in Vietnam? Don't you have something better to do with your money?"

"Agreed, point well taken, but you Brits are all mixed up in shooting civilians in Belfast—not very productive."

The man shrugged. "We were a worldwide empire for centuries and have developed bad habits. We still need someone to pick on now that we've lost our luster after World War II.

"You used to pick on us," I said, "but we took care of that now, didn't we?"

"As well you should have, and now we have a whole other mess in Bangladesh."

"Yes," I said, "and the way you partitioned Pakistan and India wasn't exactly a stellar foreign policy strategy."

The man raised his mug, "Why don't we just toast to imperialist powers that don't know any better? And this guy Nixon, he's one piece of work, like his war on drugs. Talk about barking up the wrong tree."

I nodded. "Tricky Dick is not a pleasant presentation of America. We have better citizens than him."

"Amen," the man said, and we clicked mugs.

He drained his mug and motioned to the bartender. "One more for me and one more for our Yankee guest so he can learn to appreciate a Guinness."

"Thanks, I guess you Brits aren't as stuffy as some say."

"We can be plenty stuffy and reserved when called for," the man said, "but we give you Yanks a break. You don't have a good sense of humor."

"Agreed, British humor is indeed a step above ours."

After leaving the bar, I had a chance to talk with others, and most were broad-minded. However, I didn't understand their relationship to a monarchy and their Queen, so ideologically opposed to what I thought a democracy was. Still, the roots of our less pretentious and class-oriented way of governing dated back to George Washington, who wanted to be referred to as Mr. President rather than Your Majesty.

Although superficially, the British were friendly, I thought it might be hard to get to know them. Maybe it was their long and many times cruel colonial legacy that left them reserved and sometimes suspicious of others of different cultures.

On to Paris

I left London at 7:30 p.m. and made it to Dover at 11 p.m. Finding rides was effortless.

I arrived north of Dunkirk, France, around 4 a.m. and had not slept well on the ferry. It was a gray morning, cold and drizzly. I made a sign with the word *Paris* written in large letters and sat on the side of the highway while dozens of motorbikes whizzed by inches away. I saw snails and slugs as big as my footprint. Nobody stopped, so I walked about five miles. I had only traveled a short distance but was exhausted and depleted from lack of sleep. I sensed a premonition that this might be a more arduous journey than my last adventures in Europe and hitching across the US.

Then a car stopped. A Frenchman named Pierre, wearing dark trousers and expensive leather shoes, offered me a ride to Paris. He drove me to his family home, where we delighted in lunch and supper. He even provided me with a room and a warm, comfortable bed to stay in for the night.

That evening, Pierre asked, "Where are you from in America, and can you tell us anything about your life?"

I pondered for a moment and then said, "I grew up in a suburb of New Jersey, ten minutes from New York City. My dad is a comedian and does a great imitation of Maurice Chevalier. As I grew up, I was exposed to an atypical group of adult role models, comics, and other entertainers."

Pierre's wife asked, "How has being surrounded by entertainers during your childhood affected you?"

I tried to explain: "The unusual behaviors and interactions I observed might have sparked my interest in interpersonal relations and psychology."

"Can you offer some details?' Pierre asked.

I thought for a few seconds and said, "Back in the fifth grade, I was playing ping-pong with a close friend named Fred. I remember saying to him: 'Tell me some things you don't like about me, and I'll tell you some things I don't like about you.' I thought this exchange of viewpoints would lead to a broader understanding of my positive and negative traits. I didn't realize I had my first encounter group experience. Unfortunately, the feedback we gave each other was critical. We decided it best to hold off on these types of conversations."

Photo of my parents, sister and me

Pierre agreed. "Sometimes even the best advice can come off as insensitive criticism. We French are proud people and the Parisians are even more proud, sometimes too proud. Many of them speak English but pretend they don't. However, they appreciate if you try to speak French and will likely be friendlier if you make an effort."

"I love how your language sounds," I said.

Pierre replied: "Yes, it rolls off the tongue nicely, even if not as nicely as Italian."

"Looks like you have a good balance in your life."

"Yes, our workdays are not so long like in America, and our women enjoy the value of the feminine role in the family and prefer not to take on too many responsibilities at work."

"That is changing in the U.S. with the women's movement."

"And so you know," Pierre said and poured red wine into his glass. "When the French know each other, they kiss on the cheek to say either hello or goodbye. Also, use only first names when having a conversation. We use *"Vous"* as a form of formal address, and *"Tu"* is meant only for close friends."

"Okay, thanks for letting me know. You've been a great host. Maybe one day you'll visit the U.S., and I'll show you around New York City."

Pierre chuckled. "Qui...that would be very nice."

The next day, I wandered around Paris and the Latin Quarter, continuing to meet Parisians. I walked into a dark bookstore café illuminated by the dim light from the glass doors.

I slung my backpack over a seat's backrest next to a formally dressed patron in his mid-twenties. He was short, heavily built, and wore an expensive suit with a silver tie. His attire seemed like it was meant as a disguise. I introduced myself by saying I was from the U.S. and was making my way to India. I learned that Jean was a salesman, who would shark almost anyone because, as he said, "You can't make money unless you're a player that knows how to play the game." He had spent some time in the U.S. and spoke relatively good English in a hoarse voice, not unlike a bike ride on a gravel road.

Early in our conversation, Jean let me know how he felt about my countrymen: "Americans with their heads up their ass!—deluded religious hypocrites with no redeeming values, liars, schemers, immoral con-artists!"

Reading the shocked expression on my face like *The Paris Gaz*ette, he calmed down and asked me: "Tell me about your trip; meet anyone interesting?"

I told him about a security guard at a London bank, saying, "A genuine smile met every person who walked through the door. Despite the mundaneness of the position, he seemed to carry meaning, purpose, and—"

"Fuck that! You just saw him smiling," Jean interrupted. "You don't know what the hell he thought—you're creating this fake reality."

"Sometimes it only takes one look to know something deeply," I responded, barely getting a word in edgewise.

Jean's face began turning red with outrage: "Pure bullshit! Nobody is happy as we're all addicted, addicted, addicted—exercise addictions, sex addictions, you name it! We want more resources, so we have less time to think. If we stay busy at all times, we won't feel pain. That's the lie we tell ourselves—at least I know the pain and don't use opiates to mask reality."

Bewildered by the energy of his negativity, I paused to consider what might have been at the root of these feelings. Traveling requires many skills, perhaps none more important than curiosity and empathy. I gathered the courage to face his anger directly and pry away at the pain he mentioned. Stumbling over my words, I managed a meager, "How're things going with you?"

Jean told me his dad had just died after a long, isolating stint at a nursing home, and then said: "A social, active man in his prime, he lost the ability to walk, followed by his teeth and eyesight. Telemarketer calls were the only things he had to regularly look forward to, and even then, his typical response was to fight them tooth and nail."

"Cornered and caged, a once vibrant animal died a shriveled vegetable surrounded by the constant sirens of ambulances. No different than waiting to be exterminated," Jean mumbled to the floor.

"At the cemetery, right before my dad was buried, he was powdered with makeup to create a peaceful expression on his face as if trying to make us think the dead haven't died. I saw him buried with dirt shoveled on his coffin. One day we're all gonna collapse into a dark hole. No way to avoid it; we're doomed."

Searching in the silence for anything at all to change the tone of this conversation that I had started, I offered the story of my grandmother, who predicted the sound of a bell would accompany her passing. At the nursing home weeks later, a bell sounded down the halls. She squeezed my hand and was gone.

"Just because you didn't see where the sound came from doesn't mean it didn't come from somewhere," Jean retorted before accusing me of confounding witchcraft.

Changing tactics to something inarguably optimistic, I discussed my interest in Buddha's search for enlightenment by reciting a passage from Hermann Hesse's *Siddhartha*:

"...there is one thing that this clear, worthy instruction does not contain; it does not contain the secret of what the Illustrious One himself experienced—he alone among hundreds of thousands. That is what I thought and realized when I heard your teachings. That is why I am going on my way...to leave all doctrines and all teachers and to reach my goal alone—or die."

Jean explosively reacted, "What! That figures! This guy's going to die, or they'll commit him to an insane asylum."

I countered, "This is about one of the greatest sages in the world, the Buddha, who has millions of followers throughout the world."

Jean responded, "The absolute irony of this bullshit! He says all the stuff about other teachers being phony, but can't you just hear him saying, 'Find your own goal, but be sure to pay me as your guide.' Whenever someone says he has the truth, I run in the other direction."

I jokingly said, "Maybe you should start your religion."

Jean was grinning as he said, "Oh yes! I already thought of this. It will be based on five commandments: One: Run like hell if anyone says he's god. Two: Don't believe anything except if it was told to you by Socrates, and of course, he's dead, so you don't have to worry about this. Three: Make nice to the worms as, eventually, they are going to eat you. Four: Whatever you learned in school is worthless crap. Five: Don't trust anyone; they will only betray you. Would you like to be my disciple? I'll call you Paul."

Scratching my head, I replied, "Don't think that's a religion for me."

Without pausing, Jean went on, "Why do people love to see someone beat to a pulp in boxing? Just like watching the gladiators—isn't there irony in a society where we love seeing others suffer; revel in it? Don't you get it? Look at it from a larger context. We're a mean, vicious, aggressive species. Human beings feed on misery."

"I don't agree, and you can even look at ancient cultures to see this."

"Bullshit, liberals positively portray ancient cultures...but it's not true. In ancient cultures, there were gross atrocities violating basic human rights, like discrimination, slavery, and even child abuse—just concede that humans will be the endangered species in the future."

"Anything's possible."

Jean talking over me again: "Don't you see, we want to have money, health, be successful, have others like us, and on and on. Your Buddha says he can't ever satisfy all these wants."

I fired back: "Right, our minds are like a group of monkeys, chattering away about disappointments for not getting their needs met."

Jean nodded and continued, "What's the goal of this Buddhist path? I've seen Buddhists who just sit around for hours meditating. They get glimpses of nothingness, a sore back, and painful knees. I knew a woman who meditated so much she needed a knee operation to deal with the pain, but she didn't have the money."

Feeling a bit drained, I tried one more time: "Buddhists say if you only live for attachments to things, this will set you up for disappointment and pain."

Jean responded, "What! Shit fuck. Ya know, desires are the only thing I have. Without my coffee in the morning, my paper in the afternoon, and a few other life comforts like cigarettes, I'd have cashed in my chips a long time ago. Life chews you up and spits you out."

I had no response to this. There were a few seconds of an awkward pause, and then I blurted out, "Don't you have any dreams, any goals?"

Jean seemed to smile, calmed down, and reflected, "Guess I'm still tired of living but also fear dying, but something in me keeps rolling along. Maybe in some sick, perverted way, my religion or whatever the fuck you call it might be to make people feel better. Anyone who hears my confused, psychotic ramblings must realize that as bad as things are, it'd be worse if they were me."

I was initially taken aback by Jean's attacking style, shocked by his crudeness, alarmed by his self-destructive behaviors and comments, and upset as a number of his critical statements were aimed at me. But I slowly began shedding those feelings.

I had to admit that I was amused by his irreverent and outlandish attacks on conventional beliefs and supernatural forces. I tried to appreciate Jean's spontaneity, his verbally outrageous behaviors, and his whimsical life energy.

I ended the conversation by saying, "Thanks for sharing with me." I picked up my backpack from the wooden chair, and put it over my shoulder. "Guess I'll keep rolling along too," and left through the café glass doors

This became my trip's second spiritual lesson. I realized my voyage ultimately involved trying to understand some of the aggressiveness manifested in Jean. I wondered why Jean was bitter and cynical. I realized that if people are filled with anger, spiritual growth is unlikely until they first deal with the cause of their rage.

EXPERIENCING SACREDNESS: A PSYCHO-SPIRITUAL JOURNEY

I went to the outskirts of Paris, hoping to find a ride. I had heard many travelers were struggling to hitchhike in France. I stood for two hours in the rain and fog of Paris when Louis, a middle-aged French pilot, pulled over and picked me up for a ride out of town.

We drove for nearly 200 miles and spoke few words because Louis was preoccupied with listening to a soccer match on the radio. When we reached a café, Louis offered to pay for my meal. While we ate, I overheard a conversation between two young women sitting at a table beside us. Ruth and Mary were traveling across Europe for the summer and, like me, had recently graduated from college in the U.S.

Next Stops: Switzerland and Italy

When I learned Ruth and Mary were going to Geneva, I asked if I could get a ride. Ruth and Mary were happy for me to join them, and after lunch, I thanked them and said goodbye to Louis. As we settled into the drive to the Alps, from behind the wheel, Ruth asked, "What's your religion?"

"I grew up in a Jewish community, which probably influenced my interest in trying to change the world."

"Can you tell me how Jews describe God?"

"A Jewish God is formless, all-powerful, and compassionate. While Jews cannot be gods, some Jews believe they can be god-like when they help others. The great social ethic of my religion required me to make the world a better place to live in and to prevent another Holocaust."

At dinner, we ate cheese fondue spiked with liquor. As I dipped my bread into the heated cheese, I was satisfied, warm, and content. An inebriated man from Germany joined our table. He proceeded to tell us he did not like to work but loved America because of our pornography, sexual freedom, and rampant permissiveness. We laughed at his loud assertions, and I felt my cheeks grow warm from the booze and jovial nature of the Swiss atmosphere. But we soon decided to leave as the German began to make unwanted advances on Mary, and we got up from our table against his protestations.

Ruth and Mary paid our bill since I did not have Swiss money. We drove through the valley as the night sky turned black, surrounded by tall mountains, a few with snow still at their peaks.

Our headlights cut across the dark mountain road, and I mentioned the conversation I had in Paris with Jean, hoping to hear what Ruth and Mary thought of him.

"He sounds like a troubled person," Ruth said as she stared toward the road.

Mary looked over the seat at me and added, "Also, very angry."

I considered their observations and replied, "Wish I knew why he was so troubled."

Mary replied, "Maybe life dealt him some real tragedies."

"Could it be the declining health and death of his dad?"

Mary leaned back. "And I suppose when we have these types of experiences, we can either grow from them or we can let them make us bitter and angry. I knew a mother who lost her child and never recovered. Her twelve-year-old died of cancer. You can't make sense of that."

I nodded in agreement. "If one believes in a Christian heaven, I guess a mother could say she'll be reunited with her child once she dies. If she believes, as Buddhists do, in reincarnation, that's another way to handle such a tragedy. But if you think this life is all there is and it has been extinguished for one so young, it is harder to figure out death's meaning. I guess that is what I am searching for. What is the meaning of it all?"

Ruth said, "Maybe a person can be attached to someone, but also allow the attachment to go and appreciate the time they had with the person."

Her comment caught me in an unexpected way, "I know I can't be like that, but maybe there's a way to get there spiritually."

As we drove further into the landscape, Ruth pointed outside. "Wow, look at those mountains ahead. They have been here for millions of years. Let's open our windows."

Image by Denise Hastert under Creative Commons Attribution-Share Alike 4.0 International

We rolled our windows down and felt the breeze come through like a burst of electricity. The air was clear and fresh. The car grew silent as we absorbed the breathtaking sights in front of us. Here was a utopian atmosphere, with one gorgeous snowy peaked mountain after another surrounding small villages and medieval old towns.

That night, as we drove, I slept peacefully in the back. When we arrived in Geneva, I said my goodbyes to Ruth and Mary.

Ruth said, "I hope you find an answer. And if you do, be sure to let me know."

"I'd be happy if I figured out what my question was," I said, and we all laughed.

She handed me a postcard with her address on it and got back in the car. I waved goodbye to the two women who'd been so kind to take me to Geneva, and in my limited French, I wrote on the postcard: *Et le jour est joli. Et je suis heureux. Et tous et bien.* (And the day is pretty. And I am happy. And all is well).

The people in Switzerland were more relaxed than the proud British and more friendly than the Parisians. Geneva is located in the southwestern corner of Switzerland and is known for having the headquarters of many international organizations, including the United Nations. I walked along the banks of Lake Geneva, Europe's largest lake, and met Maria, a brunette with kind brown eyes. I smiled and said hello, and she reciprocated. We ended up having coffee and pastries at a tiny coffee house managed by an older lady who shuffled about slowly and mumbled under her breath,

"Tell me about your country."

"Well, we have three official languages, German, French, and Italian. We also have one of the best healthcare systems in the world but, it's expensive to maintain."

"The U.S. has a miserable health system; it's all about the money."

"That is sad," Maria said. "My countrymen appreciate honesty and tolerance, and punctuality is a critical part of our society. It's also considered rude to stand too close when talking to a fellow citizen. It's best to stand at least an arm's length apart."

"In America, we say, 'don't get in my face.'"

Maria chuckled. "We place great importance on good manners, and most interactions are rather formal. Even schoolchildren shake hands when they meet in the street."

"Maybe that's why Switzerland is neutral and was able to survive WW II without so much as a scratch," I said.

Maria laughed. "That, and the fact that other countries trust us with their money."

We parted ways with a hug. Geneva was as civilized and opulent as I'd imagined.

I got a ride to Interlocken and Wassen, and slept in a park that night. I awoke at 1 in the morning, feeling far away from everything. I walked to the roadside and sat by the pavement at the entrance to a deserted highway. At daybreak, a German driving a van stopped to offer me a ride and drove me to Milan. Bruno, a rotund fellow with rosy cheeks, taught me some German expressions: *Ich* ("I"), *zee* ("you"), and *zimmer* ("room").

We talked about the Berlin Wall and how Bruno hoped it would one day come down and lead to the reunification of Germany. I couldn't imagine that happening anytime soon.

Then he asked, "Were you ever interested in getting more involved in politics?"

"Maybe. During the Presidential campaign of 1964, I volunteered to help at the local headquarters of the Johnson-Humphrey ticket. Two years later, because of my excellent reputation as an envelope sealer, I was asked to be the chairperson for my congressman's Young Citizens for Helstowski campaign. I jumped at this opportunity to help organize youth to distribute literature, participate in parades, and sponsor fundraisers. Both Johnson and Helstowski did win their elections, although I would not attribute much personal responsibility for either of these victories. Unfortunately, these two experiences had unpleasant longer-term outcomes. Johnson ultimately and hopelessly enmeshed our country in the Vietnam quagmire, and my congressman would later be a target of a federal corruption investigation."

"Did that end your involvement in politics?"

"My last political involvement was with the Robert Kennedy presidential campaign of 1968, and his tragic death was another crushing disappointment. Politics as a future profession became less glamorous, and my interests shifted to psychology."

"Politics is an evil animal," Bruno said while we drove through magnificent landscapes with glaciers sparkling from mountains 14,000 feet tall. We were curving down the steep terrain, while Swiss music on the radio played in the background. Later, my German friend dropped me off in the center of Milan.

With a pack on my back, exhausted, without a map of the town, the hot Italian sun blazing, I lay under a tree to rest. I made a few attempts at meeting people but was unsuccessful due to the language barrier, as they only spoke Italian. I needed the local currency to buy food. I suddenly noticed three young men dressed in scraggly jeans and sporting long hair set in ponytails. Still practicing my new smiling attitude, I walked up to them and asked, "Can you guys exchange ten dollars for Liras?"

They smiled, and Mike, who was from the U.S., said, "We don't have enough liras."

"Okay, how much you got?"

They dug in their pockets and came up with crumpled bills that added up to about seven U.S. dollars.

"That helps, thanks."

"Where are you going to?" Mike asked

"India."

He laughed. "That's funny."

"No, really, I'm hitching to India."

His smile faded. "Long hair in America and here is okay but in Kazakhstan, not so good."

"So you think I should get a haircut?"

"Maybe that's better."

"You know Crosby Stills Nash and Young?" I asked.

"Sure, good music."

"Well, they have a song called Almost Cut My Hair with David Crosby singing. It's about him thinking of cutting his hair but deciding not to because if he would, he'd be doing it to conform, would be doing it out of fear."

"That's a good song," Mike said, "but he's not hitchhiking to India."

I smiled. "You're right, but I'm gonna take my chances."

"Okay," and he reached out to warmly and firmly shake my hand. "We wish you a good and healthy trip."

"Thanks, man, much appreciated."

I tried to leave the center of Milan, and hitching was not successful, but finally, a boy helped me get out of the city when he gave me a ride on his cycle.

I found my way to Bregano, a sleepy little village nestled between ripening wheat fields and scattered groves of Elm and evergreens. It was hard to believe a place as peaceful as this could exist. Still, a handful of stone throws from the bustling city of Milan, boiling with the buzz and clamor of people going about their busy lives, seemingly unaware of the bliss one could find in the nearby countryside.

Despite doing a different kind of boiling under the oppressive rays of the summer sun, I took solace in the knowledge that I was bearing witness to a scene few would ever see, and even fewer would take the time to appreciate. The occasional blessing of a breeze would caress my worn skin before rippling through the nearby grain, bending it to and fro to become a golden sea beneath the Alps.

I rose from the gentle grass and went southwest after a three-hour rest. Fortunately, it took less than an hour of hitching for a gentleman named Luca to pick me up. While we zipped along the winding country roads, he asked me to help practice his English. Normally, I would be more than happy to do so, but as Luca swerved around while passing horse-drawn wagons and equally impatient drivers, I found it difficult to focus on the conversation. In time, my nerves settled, and I found an unlikely companion in my crazed chauffeur.

We started off our English workshop in traditional fashion while he pointed to passing objects, and I said, "Horse and wagon; beehives; meadow." His Italian accent was rolling and slow.

"How you say when you have no fun?" he asked.

"No fun? Like when you're bored?"

"Si, when having nothing to do?"

"Yeah, you're bored, that's with an e and d at the end, but we also say board with and a and d at the end, like a piece of wood or a boardwalk."

He chuckled. "Piece of board is like person have no fun."

"Yes. A piece of wood is one piece, but we have the same word, peace, which means getting along, like peace and love, the hippie slogan."

"Si, make love, no war."

"Exactly. Why can't we all just get along?"

He laughed. "With you, my teacher, I learn to speak English good."

"You'll learn to speak English well, which will make you a good English speaker."

He puffed his cheeks and widened his eyes. "English hard."

"Better if you say English is difficult. A piece of wood is hard."

He laughed and pointed to an intersection coming up. "Milan this way. I go this way," and pointed left. "Thank you for English lesson."

"It's been my pleasure; thanks for the ride."

Luca sped off into the approaching dusk. I was in the middle of nowhere when twilight turned into a dark, moonless night. Now alone without a light in a country where the landscape and language were foreign to me, I trudged on into the dark.

My luck held when I flagged down a passing van. A motley trio were they, two from Germany and one from France, all making their way to the fabled "floating" city of Venice for a bit of relaxation during an otherwise uneventful summer holiday.

Antoine, the fellow from France, served as my weak translator, as the other two occupants of the van would've made Luca's English appear almost fluent. I tried sharing a few travel stories with the lads, but Antoine got lost in translation. My anecdotes were received with polite smiles and respectful head nods. I was also tired and hungry. I hadn't eaten in many hours, and my stomach was growling with rebellion.

They finally pulled off at a rest stop for fuel and a pizza. I bought a slice.

At a glance, the shamelessly flaccid triangle of bread and cheese would appear unappealing to some, with the curiously crimson sauce and the singular paper-thin slice of pepper for garnish. For me, it was perhaps the most delightful food to have ever graced my lips; the crust was crisp and crunchy, the mozzarella and parmesan were creamy and full-bodied, and the tomato and herb blend beneath was a feast for the senses. Perhaps it was due to hunger, but that small cheesy kindness was a gift from heaven and a blessing I'll never forget.

With my belly no longer crying and the toll of my long day weighing heavily upon me, I flopped onto the rear seat and was aided into slumber by the soothing sounds of the engine and the melodious language of the three fellows.

When I awoke, I was in Venice, or perhaps more appropriately, the parking area next to it. The trio was gone, but fortunately, my belongings were not. I collected my things and climbed out of the van, making sure to lock it before making my way to the labyrinthine of alleys and canals that was Venice.

EXPERIENCING SACREDNESS: A PSYCHO-SPIRITUAL JOURNEY

I soon found myself absentmindedly wandering the street of this remarkable city, marveling at the architecture that was blessed with the beauty and the engineering prowess to continue standing above the waves below for as long as it has. Stone and wood with the trappings of Byzantine influence and the soul of the Renaissance formed the skin and bones of the towering shops and cathedrals, with a touch of character definitively Venetian. Even the humbler homes and cafes were clothed in architectural splendor.

So enraptured was I that it was perhaps an hour before I noticed there wasn't a car in sight. Most roads were too narrow for them, but those that were wide enough were equally bereft of vehicles. It was pleasant to finally explore a place as astounding and proud as this without fear of being mowed down by a rushing local, and it made the enjoyment of my time in the old city all the sweeter.

After taking my fill of the sights and a few small pastries, I mustered my courage and attempted to get a sense of what made this city so great from the people who lived there. I had been told that Venetians were shrewd and practical people, as was fitting of those descended from the merchants and sailors who'd once called this wealthy mercantile center home.

I came across an older Italian man sitting idly at a bistro and sipping the last of the red wine left in his glass. With the memory of the guard's smile fresh in my mind, I smiled at the man and asked, "Do you speak English?"

Image of Venice waterway and café under CCO.

"Si, I speak English."

"Great. Mind if I join you?"

"Is okay if you buy me more vino," and he tapped the empty glass.

"Sure, no problem," I said and sat down. "I'm Lenny, from outside New York City."

I'd realized that few knew where New Jersey was so I took the liberty to mention a city everyone knew. People loved hearing about New York City, so it was a good conversational ice-breaker.

"New York," said the man and seemed impressed. "Everybody in New York has long hair like you?"

"No, only some young people."

"Why you have long hair that look like a girl?"

"In America, it's a way of saying you don't like the government and the war."

"I no like government and war, but I no have long hair."

"Fair enough," I said when the waitress stopped by. I ordered wine for him and tea and pastry for me, "Venice is amazing. You grew up here?"

"Si, my whole life I live Venice. Venice have big history."

"For sure," I said. "Great world explorers and vast merchant ships sailed from Venice all over the world."

"Si. Venice most beautiful city in world."

"I hear Rome is nice, and Milan is amazing."

"Phew," said the old man and sipped his wine. "Venice better, mucho better."

"No place like home," I said.

"America no Columbus find," and the man frowned.

"That's true. America was first discovered by Amerigo Vespucci," I said.

He finally smiled. "Si, Vespucci Italian from Florence."

"Yup and the name America is derived from his name."

"Si," the man raised his glass. "Amerigo Italiano."

"Yes, and we have lots of Italians who immigrated to America."

He leaned back in his chair and finally lowered his guard. "Al Capone Italian but not good man. But I know one good American," he said and offered a toast.

"Thanks."

"Si, you want me buy you glass of wine?"

"Maybe another time but thanks."

The man stood up. "Me tired. Me go home sleep."

I stood up and reached out my hand. "Thanks for the company."

His handshake was dry, and his skin was layered with wrinkly old age. "Si, thank you for wine," and he wandered off down an alley.

I made my way back toward the mainland, taking every detour that caught my fancy. From what I had gleaned from my history lesson, Venice was the product of an unrivaled mix of Italian Renaissance art and Byzantine architecture that heralded back to its days as a republic, and it remained a major Italian port in the northern Adriatic Sea ever since. After seeing it in person, its monikers as the "City of Canals" and "The Floating City" hardly did it justice, what with everything else gone unmentioned, from its delicious delicacies and welcoming people to its iconic gondolas and wood-paneled water buses.

One thing of note that was not listed among Venice's many overwhelming qualities was the smell. When you were among the many stalls and cafés, you felt as if you had gone back in time to the days of the Renaissance. Still, if you wandered off the beaten path, and along one of the many intersecting canals, you'd find yourself teleported a bit further back into the Dark Ages when the air was filled with rot and mud. For all its might and splendor, Venice was a city built upon muck and low tide, a fact that became all too obvious as I finished my trek back to the parking lot.

I tried to get a ride out of Venice and was soon offered one by an Italian soldier who promised to take me to a city. My mistake was not asking "which city" before strapping myself into the seat and leaving the glittering wonders of Venice behind.

As promised, he dropped me off in a city. Which one it was, I didn't know. Short on options, I asked a bus driver for directions, which he willingly gave...in Italian. Despite our disconnect, he could sense my distress and allowed me to ride along without charge until a kindhearted person told me I was heading in the wrong direction and suggested I get off at the next stop.

I did as instructed and found myself once again at the side of the road as night descended. Thankfully, this lonely stretch of pavement had a lit bus stop and a small café, perched alongside the main road. It was an attractive place in casual ways, with wood beams and rough stone. The doorway was low, and I had to duck to pass through it.

The inn was as compelling on the inside as it was outside, smelling of wood, smoke, and wet stone as if it were a pub in Ireland instead of a tavern in Italy. I stood inside the door and looked around. Half a dozen people were scattered loosely around the room. There was no central place to wait to be seated and no staff I could see. Uncertain of the protocol I should follow, I finally sat at an open table near the small fire pit.

As if on signal, a dour waiter appeared, though not necessarily unfriendly. Without saying anything, he met my eyes, nodded, and laid a sheet of paper in front of me. I glanced at it, saw it was in the native language, and looked up apologetically.

"Water, rice, and vegetables?" I said slowly.

Without a word, he turned and soon returned with a small carafe of water and a porcelain mug, which he set on the table before me.

"Rice?" he said in a voice so laden with guttural vowels I had to think about the sounds he'd made for several seconds before the meaning became clear. I nodded and smiled, and again he turned away without any further words.

I settled back and took a tentative sip, relieved when the water tasted clear and sweet with no hint of sulfur. I looked over the others in the room, concerned not to appear to be overly curious. A group of four men, a pair of two, a single man, and myself. The group of four, all middle-aged men, wore traditional clothing, all grays and black stripes. The two men sitting separately were younger, gesticulating and arguing with one another while drinking tea in small cups.

About 20 minutes later, the scene through the window changed when a car stopped in front of the restaurant. Its long-haired occupants entered the establishment, who were loudly speaking English, much to the chagrin of everyone except for me. I practically leaped from my seat to greet them. An expression of mixed amusement and confusion flashed across their faces at finding another compatriot, albeit an overly enthusiastic one, way out in Who Knows Where, Italy.

I found out they were also traveling through Europe for the summer and had been active in the civil protests in the U.S. over the Vietnam war.

Josh, their passionate orator, opined: "It's the duty of every last American, both home and abroad, to toss themselves into the mire of politics to pursue the noble cause of casting the demon that was Nixon from office."

"Amen," said his friends.

His manifesto complete, Josh asked, "Where do you stand?

I told them I was also against the war and had participated in many demonstrations in the states. I recounted to them my trip to Washington and other activities to protest the war.

"That's cool," Josh said. "Have you considered getting into politics?"

I told them of one experience I had while a senior in high school. "My best friend Bob and I were selected to represent our town in a statewide activity that involved seniors participating in a mock legislative process at the State Capitol. Bob and I introduced a bill that would provide funds to establish a state institute to investigate the different types of drugs, including psychedelics, to find out their possible benefits or negative effects." Their eyes lit up. I was preaching to a segment of the U.S. population readily invested in my legislation.

"After introducing the bill in a congressional committee, a group of conservative mock congressmen was outraged at the idea and voted not to allow the bill out of committee. To counter this action, I approached several congressmen who agreed to the merits of this bill and subsequently joined the committee to outvote the former conservative majority. Once the bill landed in the House of Representatives, I gave an impassioned speech, but my effort wasn't enough to pass the legislation. Subsequently, I canvassed with fellow legislators and made deals to vote for their favorite projects if they'd support my bill."

"Awesome," Josh said, "what happened next?

"The strategy worked, and the legislation narrowly passed the House. Bob, the co-sponsor of this bill, was elected Speaker of the Senate. Bob and I also developed a friendship with the elected governor. With these contacts, the bill speedily passed the Senate and was signed into law by the governor. The bill received a considerable amount of press in newspapers across the state."

The guys clapped, and Josh asked, "That sounds like it went great, man."

I shrugged. "Though I successfully managed the course of the bill through the mock Congress, I found the process disturbing. To succeed, I found myself willing to make any deal to get the necessary votes. At the idealistic age of sixteen, I had already been corrupted."

Josh was skeptical. "That's how it goes sometimes, man." Sometimes we got to compromise, that's part of making change, right?"

"You're probably right; maybe I'm just not built for it."

"I for sure ain't," Josh said.

We talked, and they offered me a ride close to the border. We spoke about life, about dreams, and the hours passed quickly.

While approaching the border, the houses grew worn and dilapidated. When I bid farewell to my fellow Americans and lay my head to rest on a grass field only ten miles from my next goal: Yugoslavia.

A Narrow Escape

When I woke up, I started hitching again. I was walking along the road when I saw a huge dog standing not far away. He was black as a moonless night. His fur was short and frizzy. He had short, triangular ears that stood erect with menacing intent. His bark was deep and ominous. He took off running toward me. He lunged at my leg with his mouth wide open. He missed. The momentum carried him twenty feet past me. He turned and growled at me. If I ran, my fear would only spur the dog to be more aggressive. My only defense was to appear fearless. I continued to calmly walk along the road. The dog stood quietly, tail drooped, ears now sagging onto his head. He suddenly turned away and trotted off.

Coming so close to real danger was a jolt, and I felt energized and vital as if a veil had been lifted. The world seemed more vibrant and alive. Why did this frightening event have this effect? Did I need to be shocked by a wild dog into having a more sacred appreciation of what was always in front of me, the air, wind, sky, and water?

That reality is always there but often seems hundreds of miles away. Could I find a way to stay in that altered state for longer periods? I wondered if having a few moments of being fully present each day was what I needed to find the meaning and satisfaction I was searching for on this journey. I also wondered what had made this dog so violent and aggressive toward me.

Chapter 3: Meeting a Remarkable Stranger

Getting Ready for the Middle East

I awoke in a gravel field in Italy with one eye shut. Sleep had been restless and uncomfortable. As the sun rose, I wiped my face of the morning dew and felt my eyelid was puffy and raw, double its normal size, likely from a bug bite. I imagined I looked like I'd lost a ten-round fistfight. My body felt broken but I was up and on the road at 5 a.m., walking with my pack slung over my back until a truck driver pulled over and offered me a ride. He only spoke Italian, so we sat in silence, listening to the tires beneath us as we drove toward the Yugoslavian border.

Later, we bid each other farewell as I hopped out of his cab. The swelling on my face had finally subsided. I looked around the desolate landscape with no idea where to go next. I spotted a small store in the distance and figured this was as good a bet as any to try and find directions to the border.

No one in the store spoke English or French but after much miscommunication and wild hand gestures, I finally hitched out of the town in a car with a Frenchman in what turned out to be the wrong direction, and away from the Yugoslavian border. I got out of his car, headed in the right direction, and hitched to the border town. After crossing the border with no difficulties, I changed some dollars into the local currency and bought a cheese sandwich for lunch.

Surrounded by rolling hills of green vegetation, I was enchanted by the remarkable beauty of the countryside. With a blazing sun overhead, I walked further into Yugoslavia. I heard a man shouting, "Hoy, hoy," in the distance. He appeared to be waving to me.

He stood at a gas station with three truck drivers who watched me approach, like an apparition across the grassy fields. I walked up to them and one of them, a burly and bearded fellow, asked, "You hitchhiker?

"Yes, on my way to Istanbul."

He pulled a flask from his coat pocket. "You want Vodka?"

"No thanks, but can you help me get to Istanbul?"

An unintelligible murmur passed through the ranks and a skinny man with a mustache said, "I go Kabala, is on way to Istanbul."

"That's great, thanks."

The road was uneven with rocks and bumps for the next 150 kilometers, but the driver did his best, in broken English, to make the journey as pleasant as he could, telling jokes I couldn't understand and honking his horn at the peasants, the horses, and donkeys in the fields along the roadside. Their day was full of work, stooped over and busily tending to their crops. The loud and cantankerous vehicle charging up the road was met by many raised hands and hellos from these farmers and workers. I tried to follow the driver's conversation but ended up dozing off despite his honking.

When we finally arrived in Kabala, I thanked the driver for his kindness in giving me a ride. In front of me was a seaside resort built into the side of a mountain overlooking the Aegean. My eyes met with soft white sand, rocky beaches, peaceful nature, and olive trees. The rolling tide rushed the shoreline and met with sloping hills that became mountains. I was struck by the relationship between land and water and how they came together at the apex of a small fishing and resort town.

Several miles into town, I passed the Savina Serbian Orthodox Monastery, consisting of three churches, with a view of Mamula, an uninhabited islet in the Adriatic Sea. My mind was clear as I gazed. I was taken by the stark contrast between my morning's gravel bedside and the now green and blue seascape.

Image by Lessormore of Savina Monastery under Creative Commons Attribution-Share Alike 4.0 International

When I tried to buy two peaches for my lunch, the merchant mistakenly gave me eight. I gladly paid for them despite my light wallet, and devoured the sweet and pungent delights, fully ripened from the sun's rays. Butchers cut and cured their meats on the sides of the town's narrow streets where other vendors sold woven and handmade goods. The villagers eyed me with curiosity and mild amusement. I returned their grinning and confused looks with a smile.

EXPERIENCING SACREDNESS: A PSYCHO-SPIRITUAL JOURNEY

After walking three hours in short pants and an undershirt, I searched for a shady place to rest, as the sun had grown blinding. Several people on the road waved to me as I sat under a shady tree. A police sergeant walked over and checked on me while I rested. He was pleasant but our conversation was lost to misinterpreted words and we both decided to wave goodbye.

It was hot and dusty as I lurched off the road. I ineffectively wiped my brow with my dirty sleeve. I desperately needed some water. I saw what looked like a ramshackle café ahead of me. An elderly man was sitting at a table close to the road, with several trees separating him from the road. He shouted what I thought were warnings to stay away, as he was swinging his arms in a sweeping path, but I sensed that he wanted me to approach. As I got closer, I noticed other people sitting at this outdoor café, all enjoying the summer weather.

The man appeared to be in his 80s, about 5 foot 2 inches, and bald with a goatee. He was ancient and wrinkled, wearing faded but clean overalls. When I was about 10 feet from his table, he pulled out a chair, pointed to it, and signaled with his hand for me to sit at his table. As I sat and looked into his eyes and weathered face, I felt a strong connection even though he spoke quickly in his native language.

He reached over and touched my face with shaking hands, then pulled me forward and kissed me on both cheeks. I sat frozen. Maybe this was some sort of welcoming custom.

He reached into his pocket, pulled out a tattered leather wallet, and reverently displayed a faded photo. He spoke to me in a cracked wheeze. The other patrons all stared oddly at him.

He relaxed and smiled as he spoke, "Zivko! Zivko!"

One of the customers came over and whispered some words into his ear. It sounded a bit like Russian. Maybe Serbian? That's what they spoke in this area.

The customer looked at me and explained the exchange in halting English.

"This man say you look like dead son Zivko. Maybe you related Zivko?"

I shook my head slowly, with as much compassion as I could muster.

I replied gently as he began to cry and wipe his eyes.

" I'm not Zivko. Not your son. I'm an American tourist. I'm so sorry..."

Another whispered exchange, and the two Serbians nodded in sad, reluctant understanding.

"This man say he buys lunch you. Because you give gift him; he sees son Zivko one last time. Ok?"

The waitress returned and placed a large plate with two large pieces of bread and a pan holding six cooked eggs on the table. He placed the plate before me, gave me a fork, and insisted that I eat it all. The kind elderly man and I periodically toasted, and I forced the sour-tasting beer down my throat.

He grabbed my hand and gently pressed it. With his other hand, he wiped an errant tear away that had escaped from his reddened eyes. He started to wheeze, raised his glass of beer, upended it, and roared a message to the entire café which I did not understand.

Everyone responded with the same message, upended their glasses, and slammed them on the table. I was still bleary-eyed from the sour-tasting beer, but I took another small sip and choked up again. Everyone roared with laughter.

After about a half hour, my benefactor handed money to the owner of the café. He was helped to his crutches and shouted some farewell words as he departed in a taxi. I finished a lemon soda that the café owner had placed before me.

A person who spoke some English and who had been at the outdoor café came up to me. "You had an effect; not seen this happen before. Thanks for being nice to sit; important for my friend."

As I stood by the table and watched this second man leave, I was overcome by the gravity of this emotional experience, and I was grateful to have been able to provide some comfort to Zivko's father. The loss this father must have felt was present in his eyes, though I did not understand the words he had said to me during our lunch. We were both present and alive and together at that moment; me, a mere mirage of his son, and maybe this image was all he needed to be able to say goodbye.

I thought about the losses he had encountered and also the losses I would experience one day. I pondered what it would be like to get older, and realized that how I spent my upcoming years would influence my experiences when I was Zivko's father's age.

I understood this man at the roadside café despite our inability to communicate through words. Similar to my experience at the British bank with the bank guard, I knew something special and spiritual had occurred, as if time had stopped and I had entered a different dimension, one where judgment, criticism, or evaluation were not present, a dimension where acceptance was the only action and the only solution. I felt warm and alive from this encounter like I had rarely felt before.

LENNY JASON

Mrs. Trapp

As I continued to walk, I recalled a similar experience with an elderly person I'd encountered in college. I was volunteering at a nursing home and got to know Mrs. Trapp, an elderly woman who was confined to her bed in a supine position. In her former life, she was an accomplished and literate French scholar who traveled the world and often spoke about the world's ways and why people did the things they do. Her days at the nursing home were spent with only a few people who would visit and sit in her beige room while she stared at the ceiling and spoke about her yesterdays. Though she was filled with wisdom and insight, the staff was oblivious to her talents and gifts, seemingly from another life.

Mrs. Trapp would say to me, "Lenny, I'm at the end of my life and I'm okay with this. I have few expectations of the afterlife and am grateful to have lived as long as I have. I'm blessed with many memories. Thank you for letting me share them one last time."

"It's entirely my pleasure," I said.

She smiled through her discomfort. "I'll always remember scaling the Eifel Tower on my 25th birthday. It was a drizzly day with clouds so low, that they obscured the tip of the tower. I was slowly engulfed by the mist as I scaled the stairs (which I preferred to the elevator) and when I reached the top as if by design, the clouds drifted off and the city below me was bathed in sunlight."

"Hopefully one day I'll get to scale the Eifel Tower, and I'll remember you when I do, though, to be honest, I plan to take the elevator."

She taught me about letting go. She lived a full life, and her last days were spent in a hospital bed, facing the ceiling awaiting whatever next happened to her.

I was angry whenever I left her room. I wanted a better end to her life's journey than being laid up alone in a cold, sterile room. I was happy to see Zivko's father was still able to walk to the café, interact with others and spend his life's twilight surrounded by his community. I failed to understand why our western society built such inhumane nursing home settings and allowed for the callous treatment of our elderly – those who need to be honored and remembered for their life's work.

Continued Good Luck with Hitching

I next hitched a ride with a young Australian couple, Richard and Lucy. Richard was tall and slim, with blue eyes, and Lucy was a slender brunette with dark eyes and dimples in her cheeks—a handsome couple they were.

Shortly into the drive, Richard said, "I think Lucy likes you."

"I beg your pardon?"

He laughed. "She likes you." He turned to Lucy. "Don't you love?"

Lucy smiled. "He's cute in a studious way. Do you like him?"

Richard hemmed. "Not my type but if you want, I'll make an exception."

Lucy turned to me. "Would you care for a threesome?"

"I beg your pardon?"

Richard laughed. "Now you're embarrassing him." He turned to me. "Only if it rocks your boat."

I was finally getting a grasp on their intent. I felt the blood rush to my face. "Um...no...I mean you guys are nice but I need to stay focused on my trip to India."

They laughed, as Lucy smiled, "That's the best wiggle-out I've ever heard."

"For sure," Richard added. "No worries mate, it's all good."

"Okay...thanks..." I mumbled, beside myself.

"I'm hungry," Lucy said and pointed to a roadside café.

We pulled over, had a bite to eat, and not another word was mentioned about having a threesome. It seemed they'd forgotten ever bringing it up, which was fine by me.

We bid a friendly goodbye when we reached Belgrade, the capital of Yugoslavia, located in the north-central part of the country.

Situated on the Sava and Danube Rivers, Belgrade was at the convergence of three historical travel routes between Europe and the Balkans. The communist government nationalized most utilities and resources after WWII and by 1948, began charting a more independent policy relying on market mechanisms. I noticed a big difference between the relatively modern city dwellers and the farmers who still cut wheat with scythes and used horses. It was clear that communism couldn't compete with the western economies I'd visited. Their road to economic freedom would be a long and arduous one.

Outside of Belgrade, I saw a chartered bus with a local high school girls' basketball team. From the bus's open windows, I heard the girls shouting to the bus driver to pull over and pick up the hitchhiker. The driver pulled over and I jogged to the front. He opened the door and nodded for me to get in. Two girls waved me to an open seat and one of them, named Jana, even spoke decent English.

"Where you from?"

"Just outside of New York City."

"Why you in Yugoslavia?"

"I just finished university so decided to travel."

"What you learn in university?"

"Psychology."

I spoke slowly and paused to let Jana translate for the other girls so they could participate in our conversation.

Jana asked, "Can you tell us more about psychology?"

"Sure. Psychology lets us understand people's behavior, what brings them happiness and what brings them sadness."

Her eyes grew wide. "How can they do that?"

I smiled. "It's complicated. Ever hear of Sigmond Freud?"

"No."

"Well, he felt that it helps to talk about our feelings and about our dreams too."

"Talk about our dreams? I like to talk about my dreams, even the scary ones."

"Good. It's important to remember your dreams, maybe even write about them in your diary."

She clapped. "I have a diary. I will write about my dreams. I had a dream last night that I had ten hands. I started reading a book and a dark cloud appeared and started cutting off my hands until they were all cut. I started running and was screaming, but the cloud kept following me, and I woke up."

"Sounds scary, and not sure what it means. Thanks for sharing with me. One day when I am a psychologist, I hope to be able to figure out what these types of dreams mean." I wondered why a dark cloud was following her and how that was related to her hands being cut off. Was there some malevolent force in the world that this signified?

We talked a bit more and later I got off the bus in Nis. Jana and her friends waved goodbye from the windows while the bus chugged away in plumes of diesel.

I decided to leave Nis when I learned that it was where the first Nazi concentration camp in Yugoslavia had been located. The Nazis were a dark cloud on humanity. But I could not understand how millions of Germans allowed for the extermination of 6 million Jews. I wondered where this violence came from and how so many could be swept up in this evil. I thought of Stanley Milgram's classic psychology study that showed that most individuals are willing to follow the orders of authorities, even when they are in opposition to their values. But I also wondered if there were deeper issues that needed to be explored to find the roots of this aggression.

I walked several miles and tried to sleep in a field, but it drizzled all night. I again awoke with a swollen hand due to insect bites.

Next Stops: Bulgaria and Greece

EXPERIENCING SACREDNESS: A PSYCHO-SPIRITUAL JOURNEY

The next day I reached Sofia, the capital and largest city in Bulgaria. The oppressive heat dampened the city's activities while Arabic music played in many shops. This culture was different from the spacious, cold, agricultural northern Yugoslavia. Although Sofia had many drab communist housing blocks, it also had several spectacular ancient ruins. There were many historic and looming Eastern Orthodox churches sprinkled throughout the city.

Image by Preslav~commonswiki of St. George Rotunda in Sofia, Bulgaria in public domain

At St. George Rotunda, which had remained in operation since the fourth century, I met a visitor dressed in a Christian habit.

"Do you speak English?" I asked.

"Yes," the middle-aged man replied.

"Do you know anything about Christian mysticism?"

"It is over 2000 years old according to the gnostic texts discovered in Egypt. They stress finding the divine spark within."

"But how do they do that?"

The wrinkles on his brow deepened as he searched for the proper words. "The union with God occurs through practices and involves purging self-centeredness. It occurs by being a decent human being, loving God, and loving one's neighbors."

"But how does one do that," I asked.

"Through prayer, silence, and solitude, one can experience the presence of God. Disordered desires are stilled through prayer, watching one's breath, or repeating mantras. You should read Thomas Merton when you get a chance."

"Wow, your English is excellent. Do you have more information about Merton?"

"People in the west only feel authentic by receiving the applause of others. By detaching himself from the world and living in a Trappist monastery, he was able to find peace and gratitude by loving God and devoting himself to a life of service. He recently died."

"Sounds like he was a good man."

"He was indeed."

"Do mystics write books about their enlightenment or the state of sacredness they have reached?"

"Once reaching this state, they probably keep it to themselves or teach others. More likely, it is their disciples who write books about these visionaries rather than the person writing about their accomplishments. If one needs the attention and love of others to arrive at these states, it might signify a superfluous need for approval. But please excuse me but I now must rejoin my group."

"Sure...thanks for your time."

I'd heard about mysticism being present in some parts of the Catholic religion and hoped to read more about Merton when I returned to the states. Christians believed they could experience the presence of God through prayer. Did all religions have pathways to this kind of sacredness?

I was fortunate to soon get a ride to Greece with Franz, an older German fellow with thick graying hair and a jiggling chin who, like most Germans I met in my travels, spoke good English with a harsh accent.

Finding out I was from the states, he was quick to spark the conversation. "Lots of unrest in America."

"That would be an understatement," I said. "It's a mess."

"The chickens have come home to roost," he said.

"How so?"

"Well, when many of the population are the children of slaves, the problems build up over time."

"Yes, the legacy of slavery is a stain on our national conscience."

"How you say when the rock hits the water and makes little waves?" he asked and shaped his palm in a wave motion.

"Ripples, the ripples of slavery."

"Yes, ripples," he said with a rolling R off the back of his tongue. "Germany racist people but America racist too. It'll take a while till we pick up the pieces. Racism is a worldwide problem. The Japanese hate the Koreans, the Irish hate the English, and the Arabs hate the Jews. It's a mess."

"Big mess for Germany. Hitler bad person and make all Germans look bad. Lots of good Germans."

"I'm sure they are. Most people just want to get by and get along."

We drove in silence soaked in humanity's bloody legacy.

He dropped me off in a rural location once we crossed the border into Greece, but luckily, a bus driver saw me on the road and stopped to pick me up. The driver must have felt sorry for me or that I needed some help, but whatever the motivation, I appreciated his generous gift of a free ride into town.

Lodging that night cost 65 cents and I looked forward to finally getting a good night's sleep. A traveler advised me to take a train or bus rather than hitchhike, especially once I made it to the Middle East. I listened and nodded but my mind was made up. I'd continue hitching despite his concern.

That night I met Julia, a bright woman in her 50s from Chicago. She preferred meat and I was vegetarian. She enjoyed a cocktail while I shunned hard alcohol. Still, we found common ground when having a conversation.

"Are you familiar with the ban on abortion in the states?' she asked.

"I'm not."

"It's about a woman's right to have an abortion."

"Wow, do you think abortions will be allowed?"

"I do. Most people are leaning in that direction."

"Let me guess, the men passed the laws outlawing abortion."

Julia sipped her martini. "Yup. But the patriarchy is finally giving way. I'm so tired of stupid men controlling my life, stupid wars, greedy bastards."

"Is it any better in Europe?"

"Not really. I stopped taking the metro. Tired of getting my ass pinched."

I sighed. "That sucks. I think the men of my generation are more respectful but it'll probably take time to right the ship of sexism."

She sipped the last of her cocktail. "I'll be long six feet under when that day comes."

We sat in silence and I felt a little guilty for being a white male, the face of racism, sexism, warmongering, and religious fundamentalism.

It took a day but I finally made it to Alexandropoulos, a port and commercial center in northeastern Greece. The port's lighthouse stood at the ocean's edge and the Agia Paraskevi beach had clean and clear waters, a refreshing sight from the recent dry and craggy roads.

I strolled the beach and came upon two burly fishermen with thick beards. They stood beside a small boat that had seen better times and yelled at each other while waving their beefy arms. Visions of Melville and Hemingway came to my mind while I stood a fair distance away and watched them debate whatever issues they had. The argument finally ended when one of them kicked the hull of the boat and huffed away. The other stood forlorn but followed his friend. I concluded that, after who knows how many years of service, the boat had reached the end of its productive road.

Turkey's border was only an hour's drive away. I stood at the side of the road and stuck out my thumb. Many cars passed; none stopped. So I began walking almost ten miles to the border. As I'd been walking for miles almost every day, my feet were laden with ridges of blisters set to pop along the soles. I felt a hint of apprehension grow in my stomach as I neared the crossing between Greece and Turkey.

I met a traveler from Belgium, and we chatted and entered the border station together.

"Do you enjoy hitching?" he asked.

"It's been great. I now know what a pincushion feels like because the bugs in this part of the world are ferocious at night. I was attacked by a mad dog, sat for hours in the sun, and was exhausted from hitching, but other than that, it's been a blast."

He smiled and nodded. "Keep smiling. It's gonna get worse."

He had long hair and the guards at the border station became suspicious. They searched through all his belongings and took him to a room to continue the search. He was denied entry to Turkey because he didn't get the proper passport stamps the last time he visited.

I was allowed to continue my journey without incident.

On to Turkey and the Middle East

Hitching in Turkey on my way to Istanbul, I got a ride from Abdul, a man in his 30s from Saudi Arabia. He had a finely trimmed beard and mustache and dark, expressive eyes that I soon found out were clouded with judgment and criticism. His English was polished due to the fact he attended college in England.

EXPERIENCING SACREDNESS: A PSYCHO-SPIRITUAL JOURNEY

"You Americans are all about money and consumerism. You're a selfish people."

I could've let go and elaborated on the Saudi monarchy, just about the most corrupt and archaic dynasty on earth, but I'd by now become good at biting my tongue, partly due to the need for self-preservation (the guy could kick me out of his car and leave me stranded in who knows where) and partly because I was still trying to encapsulate the smiling guard whose lesson of tolerance I was trying to absorb.

"Not all of us, and we also invented stuff like the car, the plane, the telephone, and television."

"This is all consumerist stuff," said Abdul driving a German BMW. "You have no morals."

At this point, I could restrain myself no longer, "Oh yeah? And how about how you treat women? They can't drive. They can't vote. They can't even go to college. It's true that we need to do better, and the war in Vietnam is no good for anyone."

Abdul hunched over the steering wheel and changed the subject as he continued his tirade, now directed at the Turks. "Turkish people are stupid and careless. They will rob you blind. Be careful and keep your distance from them."

"I will try to be careful. I'm just interested in traveling and meeting new people, like you, and hearing what you have to say."

He shrugged in dismissal of my quest but remained cordial throughout the rest of the ride. I had been successful in diverting our conversation to more nuanced tones. Istanbul was an hour away.

Istanbul, the largest city in Turkey, is located in northwestern Turkey and straddles the Bosporus strait, which connects the Black Sea to the Mediterranean. The city's history is a staggering journey through human evolution. Once named Constantinople, it suffered the wrath of conquering armies, be they Greek, Roman, Huns, Christians, or Muslims. Still, there it stood resilient as ever—the gate from the east to the west.

I rented a tiny room at a hotel for sixty cents, which had four beds. There was barely enough space to walk to my bed.

The next day, strolling the narrow streets, I bought a loaf of bread for eight cents and was eating at the entrance to an alley when four children stepped out of the shadows, their small palms begging for food or spare coins.

"Mister," the tallest one said. "Mister."

They stood firm, palms upright, and the boy said again, "Mister."

I sliced my loaf in half. I handed the bread to the boy. "That's all I got."

They looked at me with pleading eyes but also sensed my improvised state. They ran off and faded into the ally's shadows.

Witnessing the poverty, unlike any in the U.S., continued to haunt me in my travels. Maybe, however obtuse Abdul was, he did have a point about American gluttony and self-entitlement. Was my well-intentioned and austere journey in search of spiritual clarity but another manifestation of Western self-entitlement?

I walked away awash with doubt but still concentrating on the job at hand.

I walked into a café and was greeted by a young waitress wearing a stained apron. She offered a faded menu. I pointed to what I thought was some kind of soup. She grinned and nodded, then motioned with her hand while she mimicked drinking from a glass and muttered something. I nodded in confused agreement as she giggled and walked off to the kitchen.

She returned with a broth that smelled sour. Traveling as I was, I couldn't be a picky eater but that soup or brew looked scary. I looked out the window and was once again amazed at history's reflection staring before me.

For over 2,500 years, Istanbul had been part of the Roman, Byzantine, and Ottoman empires. I saw breathtaking views of Ottoman palaces, Byzantine castles, and the 17th-century Sultan Ahmed Mosque, the Blue Mosque, with its grey cascading domes and six minarets.

Image by Jorge Láscar of the Sultan Ahmed Mosque (Blue Mosque) under Creative Commons Attribution 2.0 Generic

I left the soup on the table and walked out.

I spent the next morning trying to catch a ride beneath the hot sun at the edge of the city. Cars and trucks roared by and honked their horns. Pollution and haze filled the air. Several of the cars were from the 1950s and quite large, but even so, some locals still had horses pulling carts and men carrying bundles.

Barely Escaping Harm Again

The day grew progressively worse, with few drivers pulling over or even acknowledging me from their windows. I was despondent when a car sped past me. The door suddenly swung open and nearly hit me. I stepped back in the nick of time and hit the ground. I landed on a rock that hurt my lower back and sent waves of pain up my spine. I was breathless. I lay motionless and looked up at the sky. Two crows flew over me. Their angry, hoarse squawks fanned my despair and pain.

Confused and upset, I slowly regained my footing and watched the car speed off into the hazy distance. I understood in my bones that this had been a deliberate and unabashed attempt to hurt me. Why would someone do that? What is the force within some people that drives them to intentionally hurt another? How were we to be aware of these dark impulses, and what were we to do with them if they reared their hateful form?

I recalled Albert Bandura's research, which revealed that when children were presented with an adult being aggressive toward an inflatable clown - kicking, hitting, and throwing the doll - the youth were more likely to exhibit aggression themselves. By this account, simply by observing aggressive behavior from parents or others, people were ultimately destined for the potential to aggressively hurt others. But I intuitively knew there must be other deeper reasons for this violence, and part of my journey was to discover them.

Still, on the outskirts of Istanbul, two policemen approached me from their van. My stomach shrunk with dread. What laws have I broken? I was helpless, putty in their hands. Will they ask to be bribed?

EXPERIENCING SACREDNESS: A PSYCHO-SPIRITUAL JOURNEY

Both cops were stocky with thick eyebrows and dense mustaches. Their pistols hung ominously from their belts. I stood frozen, not far removed from when the dog in Italy lunged at me.

Sensing I was not Turkish, one of them asked in English, "What are you doing?"

"Trying to hitch a ride to Ankara."

"You American?"

"Yes. Is that a problem?"

"No, because Americans are stupid." The officer laughed and his partner joined in.

"Why am I stupid?"

"Because you try hitch to Ankara. You want to die?"

"I don't understand."

The officer pointed to the road stretching ahead. "Is dangerous. Why you not take bus?"

I stood exhausted, ready to pack it in when the other officer flagged down a passing bus. The bus chugged to the side of the road. The officer had words with the driver and motioned me to get on board.

I didn't resist. Perhaps public transportation would be a wiser decision from here to India.

The crowded bus housed sweaty odors of unwashed bodies: a fetid mix of rotten garlic and apricot brandy. To this day the scent of garlic brings back memories of this ride.

The driver said, "Twenty lire."

A local had told me in the streets of Istanbul to bargain in most transactions so I replied, "I only have ten."

We bargained back and forth and settled on fifteen lire.

There was an empty seat by the driver and we got to talking. I shared some of my exploits while he shared how he'd taken this job to pay for his third child.

"That's good to hear. That you have children."

He kissed the tips of his fingers. "Children very good."

He later gave me the five lire back when I departed. I traveled over three hundred miles for only a buck that day. Many of the people on the bus tried to practice their English with me, and several gave me fruit and even offered cigarettes.

A young man with a large tray of bottled drinks got on the bus and sprayed perfume into the air. Turkish music blared from a speaker.

Hour upon hour I sat, sometimes dozing, sometimes awake. My stream of consciousness wandered from one subject to the next. At times I was at peace, at other times, I wondered about the journey I'd embarked on.

We arrived in Ankara at 10 p.m.

I slept at the bus station that night and was repeatedly startled awake by Turks hoping to speak with me and inquire where I was headed, or if I had money to spare or food to share.

The next day I walked around Ankara, green and lush with more parks compared to Istanbul. A Turkish student quite fluent in English offered me food while we sat on a park bench.

EXPERIENCING SACREDNESS: A PSYCHO-SPIRITUAL JOURNEY

When I mentioned that quite a few men were walking holding hands, he chuckled. "Girls are protected by their mothers until marriage. They cannot leave the house without a chaperone. Men here are so sexually frustrated they are resigned to having sexual relations with men."

"So, they're straight men who seek intimacy with other men because they can't date women?"

He replied that it was not a good situation in his country.

That evening, I got on a bus to Erzurum. The bus pulled over every so often and all passengers got off and had tea. When we returned to the bus, a man came around again and sprayed us with perfume.

The countryside became more arid and hillier as we drove farther. It took 16 hours to get to Erzurum, a city in eastern Turkey nestled in a fertile plain 6000 feet above sea level.

I was exhausted when I got off the bus and found a hotel.

The next morning, I was greeted by many friendly people having their breakfast of bread, cheese, and tea. Several guests invited me to join them and I graciously accepted their ripe, fresh cantaloupe, salty cheese, and the crusty day-old bread, baked yesterday and crunchy from being out overnight. Everyone appeared to be in great spirits, laughing, joking, and enjoying the meal.

Later, I walked through town with a Turkish man who spoke some English, to find a currency exchange. We walked through the picturesque town, markets humming with activity, women in wide, colorful gowns shopping, vendors challenging one another, yelling out their available goods. The town clattered with horse-drawn carriages; shops housed in stone buildings that were constructed at the turn of the century; elderly women covered in veils who begged at street corners. Life pulsated around me, filled with glory and despair while a thousand spicy scents mingled in the air. I was stunned at what I saw before me, the disparity between such great beauty and harrowing poverty merely a few steps away. We finally found a place where I converted some of my money.

Money Stolen

That evening, while I ate my supper, somebody snuck into my room and stole my traveler's checks. I'd made it a habit to keep the checks in my pocket, but that night, I let my guard slip and left them in my backpack at the hotel. Murphy's Law showed no mercy.

I sat on the bed. My body felt as limp as a ragdoll. What impulse or evil instinct drives a person to take what was not theirs? Is theft simply another violent regularity of the world? This thief took from me and was not the only thief in existence. Thieves dressed as professionals in our business community lied and cheated their way to the top. Politicians often did anything and everything to win their elections. I needed to understand this aggression, these ways of the world as people struggle for meaning and survival. It was all a stupid and frustrating mess. I barely slept that night. It had been the lowest moment of my journey so far.

I had just enough money to pay for my room and for the bus fare to get me to the border. I had to keep going. The option of calling my parents crossed my mind but where would I find a phone and where would they send me money?

No. I had pledged to do this trip on my own and that was that. I thought to myself I'd get to Tehran where I'd find an American Express station that would refund my Traveler's checks.

EXPERIENCING SACREDNESS: A PSYCHO-SPIRITUAL JOURNEY

At the bus station, I went from bus to bus in search of the lowest fare to conserve what little money I had left. I finally bargained a driver down to twenty-five lire from thirty.

Waiting for the bus, I was approached by two young men with long hair, scraggly beards, faded jeans, and worn-out sandals.

"Hey there, I'm Johnny. Are you American?"

"Sure am. From outside New York City."

"Cool, I'm from Boston. This is my buddy Liam. He's from Holland."

"Nice to meet you guys," I said. "How are travels?"

Johnny replied, "So far so good. Gotta go with the flow."

Given my most recent experience with theft, I replied, "I hear that, but sometimes the flow is a gushing white river rapid."

"Ain't that the truth."

The locals stared at us. They found three white men an odd sight at their local bus station.

"They're looking at us like we're from Mars," Johnny said.

"We kinda are," Liam said. "For them. Can you imagine having to live your whole life here?"

"That would be a major bummer," Johnny said, "almost as bad as serving in the crappy U.S. army." He faked a salute.

The bus we boarded was rerouted and we stopped in a small town far from the intended Iranian border. The desert sky had grown dark and cold, a whipping and desolate wind blowing misery. We found someone with a Volkswagen van to take us closer to the border.

After hearing about the theft, they paid for my transportation, dinner, and rent for a room that evening.

During supper, Liam sipped on his tea and asked, "What have you learned from the travels so far?"

I told them of my experiences with Jean's rage and the dog attack.

Still ruminating on my stolen money, I was feeling out of sorts.

"You gotta let it go," Johnny said.

"I know. I'm trying. I'm more pissed off at myself than at the thief. What was I thinking?"

"You weren't thinking," Liam said, "and now you're thinking too much."

After we sat in silence for a few seconds, Johnny said, "Let's put things in perspective. You're alive and got all your limbs. My buddy Marty lost his legs in Vietnam. You wanna switch places with him?"

"No," I said, suddenly feeling like a spoiled brat.

"Good, so count your blessings and stop the whining."

"Okay..."

Liam asked, "Why did you want to take such a grueling journey all the way to India"

"Seeing how the rest of the world lives is probably good for me. I'm also hoping to find wisdom and meaning in the Eastern religions."

Johnny asked, "Where else have you searched for meaning?"

"I once thought the existential philosophy of understanding the universe had the answer. But this philosophy of a meaningless universe was too dark for me. And life had to be more than a long, unending struggle to push a rock up a hill, only to have it roll back down the hill and have to start all over again."

"Have you found a different philosophy?"

"That's what my journey is about. I want to find out whether Eastern religions provide a better approach."

"Anything else you are searching for?"

"Maybe. The violence I have seen has opened up a deeper search, and I'm not sure what that is about."

Liam asked, "Can you tell me more?"

"Sure, I am looking for what will bring me fulfillment and happiness in my life. I need to find out more about who I am, and what is there about the aggression I see popping up in so many places."

Johnny added, "Violence is everywhere man, and no doubting that."

"Also on my trip, I have been thinking that my life has been on overdrive for a long time. I rarely notice nature's beauty. But my inner drive to succeed is probably not unique, as many people in the U.S. struggle with this."

Johnny said, "Maybe there's a cultural orientation afflicting Western people who define themselves by how much they accomplish. A strong feature of our protestant work ethic. One's righteousness is determined by one's achievements."

I agreed and added, "In my case, there might be other psychological factors behind my drive or will to keep going, keep succeeding, and keep accruing."

Johnny asked, "Can you clarify?"

"I've been thinking about this for a while. My high school days were less hectic. I was a good student but not an overachiever. Academics didn't define my existence. But in college, I needed to be at the top of the class. Still not sure what has been driving me, but I hope to find answers."

Two Irans

The next day, we caught a bus to the Iranian border. Johnny and Liam were heading in a different direction. They were generous enough to give me a few dollars to help me get to Tehran.

We hugged and shook hands as men do. They remained a guiding light throughout my journey, and when things got rough, I'd mumble, "Count your blessings."

As I had heard, hitchhiking was nearly impossible in Iran. No one picked me up and I was soon thrown out of a trucker's area by the police. After heading to the nearest bus station, I met Thomas and William from England and Oliver from Australia. They were loud and friendly, quite the contrast from John and Liam, and when they heard my story of having my money stolen in Turkey, they also gave me a few dollars to help me get to Tehran.

The bus ride lasted all day and night. We arrived in Tehran at four in the morning. I walked the streets of the city while dawn became morning and the city awakened.

The heat in Tehran was unbearable, and many of the Iranian faces were lined with wrinkles from straining to avoid the sun's glare. Many women wore black veils, and as in Turkey, I felt like I had been transported into a distant time in the past.

EXPERIENCING SACREDNESS: A PSYCHO-SPIRITUAL JOURNEY

I was surprised to see an ancient and modern Iran. The city was wallpapered with posters of the Shah and his family. At Tehran University, I saw women students in miniskirts. Compared to Turkey, Iran was progressive, as women could enter the educational system. I was told that Tehran even had the beginnings of a modern film and television industry.

It was also apparent the royal family had created incredible social and economic inequalities, which would prove to be its demise in the not-too-distant future.

I headed to the American Express with only $1.50 left in my pocket.

Once in the office, a dark and cramped room with a low ceiling and a grumpy clerk who sipped coffee from a tall white ceramic cup, I filled out the forms with dirt under my fingernails.

The clerk reviewed the forms with a frown that knitted his bushy eyebrows. He opened a drawer and allotted me $100.

"What's that?" I asked. "They stole $500."

He waved me off. "You get the rest in New Delhi."

"What?! How am I supposed to get to New Delhi on a hundred bucks?"

He shut the drawer with a thump and gazed at me with lifeless eyes. "New Delhi."

He turned away and dedicated himself to shuffling papers that lay in a pile on his stained desk.

I stood bereft and confused. What could I do? Nothing. The guy had me over his lap with his mindless lack of concern for my well-being. I could've yelled at the top of my lungs and thumped my fist on the table. It would do no good.

I walked out in emotional disarray. The lively markets now seemed irritating.

The Holy City of Mashhad

The next day, Thomas, William, Oliver, and I spent twenty hours on the bus from Tehran to Mashhad. The ride to Mashhad was dreadful and nausea ran through our group due to food poisoning. The Iranians were building a new highway and instead of constructing one section at a time, they leveled the entire four-hundred-mile passage so we were left to use alternative dirt and rock roads.

We arrived in Mashhad at 3 a.m. and slept in a park for an hour. Later we checked into a cheap hotel.

The next morning, a teenager walked up to us and said, "I am Ali. I show you Mashhad. Only twenty lire."

It turned out to be a good deal. Mashhad is Iran's holiest and second-largest city, located in the northeastern province of Khorasan. The name Mashhad means 'place of martyrdom' where Imam Reza was killed. He was the great-grandson of Imam Ali, who was the cousin of the Prophet Mohammad. Each year, millions of pilgrims visited his tomb and shrine – a place of reverence.

EXPERIENCING SACREDNESS: A PSYCHO-SPIRITUAL JOURNEY

Image by Iahsan of the Imam Reza shrine in Mashhad under Creative Commons Attribution 3.0 Unported

We toured the Imam Reza Shrine complex, which had seven massive courtyards and a golden dome above the shrine. The large mosque was layered with blue tile and intricate Arabic calligraphy. Mashhad had many water parks crowded with thousands of pilgrims visiting the holy city, along with turbaned priests and self-flagellating ascetics. They were joined by beggars, sick elderly men, and mothers clutching babies that wailed with hunger.

We walked through narrow, mazelike streets, and encountered hundreds of men and women who were skilled artisans working from small shops tucked into the thick walls. Some sold Persian rugs, others turquoise stones. We were served tea while the merchandise was displayed for us to buy. In one shop, a young Persian man who spoke broken English asked us to help him write a letter to an American friend.

"I want to go America," he said, "but need $4000 to leave Iran."

"How come?" I asked.

"Government bad, no let us leave."

"Sorry to hear that."

The young man wiped the sweat from his brow. "I no wife with no money. Girl parents not give me girl."

"I see, you need to have money to get married."

"Yes. I go America to go university and meet America girl for sex."

I heard the sense of hopelessness in his voice, living in a restrictive and sexually repressed society. He'd probably read about the sexual revolution in the states and wanted nothing more than to belong and be free.

"I not yet kiss girl," he said with a tear in his eyes.

I helped him with a letter, but I could feel the weight of the autocratic Iranian system crushing his spine with its archaic and bygone customs.

Many little boys came up to us saying, "Hello mister". We learned from Ali, our Persian translator, that many of the smiling youngsters who were saying hello to us in English were also mocking us in Iranian, saying fuck you, still with a smile on their faces. When we stopped to eat mulberries from a street vendor, a person passing by said to make sure our dishes were separate from the others. Turns out that most Iranians believed we were dirty Christian heathens and that our plates had to be washed five times after use.

I visited a bookstore where I saw a well-groomed man in Western clothes sifting through the books.

EXPERIENCING SACREDNESS: A PSYCHO-SPIRITUAL JOURNEY

"Do you speak English?" I asked

"Yes."

"Would you mind sharing your knowledge of Islam?"

"Not at all. In Islam, we believe in the prophet Muhammed, worshipping Allah, the one God in the Ummah, which is a unified community based on the teachings from the Quran and Hadith. This worship is a spiritual guide for all aspects of life, including personal conduct and economic and political systems."

I dared to ask, "Do you find your religion sexist, as the women are covered from head to toe and obedient to the men in their lives, starting with their fathers and ending with their husbands?"

Though he did not directly address my inquiry about sexism, the man said, "We believe in the Five Pillars of Faith, and our religion forbids us to engage in any discriminatory practices. We are against liquor, gambling, slavery, prostitution, and superstition. There's no deity except Allah, we pray five times daily, we give 2.5% of our earnings to those in need, we fast during the month of Ramadan, and make a pilgrimage to Makkah at least once in our lifetime."

"Do you know much of Islam's mysticism?"

"Sufism is the mystical path."

"Can you offer more details?"

"There is no fixed practice or approach. Sufis find meaning in life approached through experiential knowledge and not through the rational mind as you do in the west. The goal is to be present in all its fullness. One of the best storytellers in this tradition is Rumi. His message is to wake up but also stay active in the world."

I wrote Rumi's name in my journal as I would later try to read his work when I returned to the states.

I wasn't feeling well that day. I was bloated and constipated from the travel and exotic foods. All I could stomach was tea and fruit. I also suspected that drinking unfiltered water contributed to my discomfort.

My queasy stomach felt better the next day and we traveled through Iran's eastern territory. Time moved quickly in our hot, jammed bus. We began to notice more Afghans dressed in their distinctive turbans and baggy, almost pajama-like, loose-fitted clothing.

Traveling Through Afghanistan

We finally arrived at the Iran-Afghanistan border. Detained for a few hours, we missed crossing that day as the Afghanistan border closed at 7 p.m. We were forced to seek food and lodging at the single-border inn.

That night, we met an Afghan who spoke German. His conversation was translated to us by another hotel guest from Denmark who spoke German and English.

The Afghan spoke and the conversation quickly turned into a breathtaking social and political diatribe while the Danish man translated: "My country is wealthy with resources but there's military suppression by the King and his army. Students are often shot when they seek education, reform, and modernization. The ruling elite wants the political and economic situation to stay the same as it's been for 500 years. Women are forced to be covered in black and men wear relics of the past. Although the elite are content and happy, many younger generations want our country to modernize. Universities were closed a few years ago, although some small schools are still open. There are fifteen million people in my country but only 1000 students."

We sat in momentary silence while two backpackers joined Thomas, William, Oliver, and me. One of them asked, in a British accent,

"Why the long faces? Who's got the hashish?"

As if from thin air, a young Afghan man walked out from the shadows and pulled out a small cloth bag tied to his waist.

"Now we're talking," the backpacker said. "Let's see the goods."

The dealer showed him a finger-long slice. The backpacker studiously smelled and felt the hash, then nodded. "Pretty fucking cool."

He bought four ounces for 25 cents and smiled at the group. "Party time."

We sat in a circle and watched a Danish guy expertly roll joints (many of the Europeans rolled their tobacco cigarettes). The joints circled the circle. I politely abstained. Clouds of thick sweet smoke rose in the air while the smokers coughed and wheezed.

"I'm now officially a nine-year-old Hindu boy," Thomas said.

Oliver laughed. "And I'm cruising comfortably at 37,000 feet."

William coughed his lungs out. "Whoever gets this shit to Europe is making bank."

Then, a thin, pale man in his 30s stood up and started groaning and pulling on his hair. "I'm not feeling good. My brain hurts." He started walking around in circles while flailing his arms and sweating profusely.

"Someone's having a bad trip," Oliver said.

William shook his head. "He's hyperventilating, only makes it worse, someone should try to calm him down."

"I'll try," I said and stood up even though I wasn't sure what to do. I walked over to the man and offered him water. "You'll be fine."

The fear in his eyes was palpable while his chest heaved with panic. "I'm scared."

"It's okay to be scared, but check it out," I pointed to the happy-stoned group. "They're doing okay so at least we know the hash is not poison. It's just good hash. You just smoked too much. I know you feel the panic will go on forever but it won't, I promise you that. Let's walk and talk and get it out of your system."

His name was Johan, from Norway, and I spent the next 30 minutes talking him down. We returned to the circle and were greeted with claps and laughter.

Johan smiled sheepishly and said, "No more hashish for me."

"We love you anyway," the British chap said. "More for us."

It remains one of the most practical applications of my academic studies.

That night, I slept on a rug. It was dirty, hot, and noisy, with many flies buzzing around my head. With little sleep, I woke feeling half-dead.

That morning we traveled to Herat, an ancient city in western Afghanistan. I was not able to travel further as I was sick as a dog. My companions continued on their journey.

I was curled up on a dusty mattress on a creaky bed when Freja, a young Danish woman with blonde hair in braids and kind blue eyes, who I met the night before, walked in and asked, "How do you feel?"

EXPERIENCING SACREDNESS: A PSYCHO-SPIRITUAL JOURNEY

"Like I've gone to Hell in a handbasket."

She chuckled. "I hear Hell is a lot of fun this time of year."

"Nope."

She placed her soft palm on my sizzling forehead. "I think you have a stomach bug." She said and handed me a canteen. "You need to drink lots and lots of water."

I sipped sparingly. "I'll try."

"Also, take these pills," Freja handed me two white capsules. "It will help your fever come down."

Freja kept a watchful eye on me and insisted I drink copious amounts of herbal tea brewed by a local medicine woman. It took me two days to break the fever and start coming back to my normal self. When I felt better, I decided to continue my trip. I was so grateful for Freja's maternal and caring tenderness that I wrote this for her:

In this godforsaken land, with rotting camel's corpses, devoured by infected mosquitoes, amidst this arid wasteland. My sight a blight of no life, a moment slammed out of eternal time. An oasis, a rest, a haven of green before me. The trees shade my parched brow. The cool water healed my cracked lips. Tis cool beneath the willow tree. The sky, the land, the green, and you. All secrets unveiled before me. And so. Thank my noble princess. For covering me with this gentle blond hair.

My bus ride to Kabul was extremely uncomfortable as the road was once again bumpy and swerved along the countryside. I traveled most of the day and into the night, arriving in Kabul at 3 a.m. The bus driver provided me with a free taxi to a hotel, which cost twenty-five cents a night. After drinking what seemed like gallons of tea, my stomach settled and I was replenished from the day's travels.

Outside the hotel, one evening, several Afghan boys were singing with a guitar. They invited me to join them. I clapped my hands to the Arabic music and felt quite groovy.

One Afghan offered me cigarettes.

"No thanks," I said, and jokingly added. "I just want hashish."

Before I could move, he sprung to his feet and dashed off. He returned with two hefty chunks of hash. "For you, no money."

I smiled with embarrassment. "I'm sorry, I was only kidding. I can't accept your offer. I hear Afghan jails are not much fun, especially for foreigners."

He shrugged. "Okay," and resumed singing with the rest of the boys.

Kabul, the capital of Afghanistan, was surrounded by snow-capped mountains and was one of the most enchanting places I had visited, with lush gardens and palaces. Although many men and women wore traditional Afghan clothing, others were dressed in western clothes.

At one of the markets, I approached a man in a more western-style outfit. "I'm from the U.S. I wonder if you speak English and have a few minutes to chat about your country."

He agreed, and we sat down at an outside café. He was a middle-aged, Afghan government employee. Our chat quickly turned to the current political situation in his country.

Image by Joe Burger of Kabul under Creative Commons Attribution-Share Alike 2.0 Generic

I mentioned, "I met a student who felt there was serious repression in your country, and that most did not have any opportunities for getting an education."

"The situation does vary in different parts of the country, but overall, this is a time of relative stability due to our monarchy, with some democratic reforms."

"Can you tell me more about these reforms?"

"Yes, Abdul Zahir has recently been confirmed as prime minister and the king respects his wishes and that of the legislators. There is an intent by the Prime Minister and legislators to help those from low-income groups. Afghan women can attend Kabul University."

I replied, "Are there obstacles to making this all work?"

"Yes, there is a serious drought affecting the country, with many crossing to Iran and Pakistan in search of food. The Afghan government is in the process of undertaking a large campaign to deal with the emergency."

I had so many more questions I wanted to ask but he looked at his watch as he had to make an appointment. I thanked him for his time and continued sitting in the café, surveying Kabul and the subtle mix of east and west in the heart of Afghanistan.

As I traveled through the middle east, I met a steady stream of tourists, hippies, and adventurers like myself. Travelers from the U.S. were more likely to limit their trips to western Europe, whereas those from Europe and Australia were more likely to make these overland trips as an initiation rite of passage to adulthood. A British man I spoke with in Kabul stated it best, "We want to challenge ourselves and see the world, and that includes countries that have customs and traditions different from our own."

It's also fair to conclude that many were attracted to these foreign lands due to the availability of hashish.

Through Pakistan

I took a bus from Kabul to the border and next traveled by train to Peshawar, the oldest city in Pakistan. It has a recorded history dating back to 539 B.C., lying just east of the historic Khyber Pass and close to Afghanistan's border. I took a train all night to Lahore, Pakistan's second-largest city, and a major center for Qawwali music. I first heard this type of music on the train. It is derived from Sufi Muslim poetry, and its intention is for the listener to experience the ecstasy of a spiritual union with God. From the train, I saw snow-capped mountains in the north and heard about sunny beaches in the south. Pakistan had many lakes and rivers, including the Indus River, and several deserts in Punjab and Sind.

The trains were crowded and mirrored a vaudeville comedy every time they stopped, with the passengers madly running to find a seat. Some travelers were ultimately relegated to sitting on the floor. With the heat of 99 degrees in the shade, I was sweating like a sumo wrestler in a sauna.

Talking to passengers on the train, I learned that there are many religions in Pakistan, including Hinduism, Christianity, Parsis, Sikhism, and Buddhism, but about 95% of the population is Muslim. It has been shaped by India, Central Asia, and Middle East cultures, and influenced by the famous Silk Road leading from China through Kashmir. Pakistan is also home to Taxila, founded in the 10th century B.C., and one of the oldest known universities in the world.

I would have liked to have spent a few days in Pakistan; however, tensions had been rising as East Pakistan moved to become an independent country called Bangladesh. Local Pakistanis mentioned that the West Pakistan military had launched a war against the people of East Pakistan while trying to eliminate nationalist Bengali civilians and armed personnel. A self-determination movement in East Pakistan had arisen to counter this genocide. It was prudent to steer clear of the war and to remain on the train as I passed through Pakistan.

As I approached India, I didn't have much energy and had developed a sore throat. Several passengers on the train told me about Kullu Valley, a refreshing place in Kashmir, and I thought it would be a good destination to visit to regain my health.

Record of My Travel Expenses to India

Chapter 4: Searching for the Buddha

―――

At Last, India

Arriving at the Indian border, I met Aayanash, an Indian who had visited many ashrams and holy places from India to Japan. His hair was thin and ran past his shoulders. He wore a five-foot-long white cotton Dhoti, with a brown belt around the waist. His dark-brown eyes projected tolerance. I walked up to him. "Hi, I'm Lenny. Do you speak English?"

"Yes, I'm Aayansh," and he smiled with his white teeth.

"What religion are you lined up with?"

"I am a Buddhist."

"Can you share what Buddhism is about?"

"Of course. Idea is death of the ego. There are Four Noble Truths to follow to achieve this."

"Can you describe them?"

"Yes. The First Truth sees life as full of suffering due to sickness, death, separation from loved ones, desire, attachment, and clinging. The cause of suffering explored in the Second Truth says attachment and desire will lead to anger, grief, and despair. The Third Truth explains that when you understand this part of life, you can cease suffering. The Fourth Noble Truth describes the path of how to eliminate suffering, and that is the Eightfold Noble Path: rightness in speech, action, livelihood, concentration, mindfulness, effort, understanding, and thought. It is possible to experience joy in a turbulent world of desire and fear. No need to judge sensations as good or bad. Simply experience the moment."

His answer to my question was concise and delivered in a quick staccato Indian accent. I found myself chasing his words, yet they made sense. I was aware of the teachings based on Buddhism and the theme that life is filled with suffering and that this suffering was due to people being attached to material things in the hope these desires would ultimately make them happy. Living in the states made it amply obvious that that wasn't the case. For if so, we would be the happiest people on Earth.

Image by Jorge Royan of Holy man with Creative Commons Attribution-Share Alike 3.0 Unported.

I was hoping to learn more about eternal truths within this ancient religion.

A man sitting next to Aayansh with white paint on his forehead and dressed in a yellow toga asked, "Would you like to play a game?"

"Sure."

EXPERIENCING SACREDNESS: A PSYCHO-SPIRITUAL JOURNEY

He smiled. "Imagine not having any biological needs. You do not need to sleep, eat, or even use the bathroom. You no longer have any sexual desires. You do not need money and have no need to work. You have all the materials you could ever want."

I smiled. "Wow, weird."

His wrinkly brow rose. "Why?"

"Well, the things you mentioned involve how I spend most of my day. I guess these are my animal needs. What would you do without any of these desires or wants? How would you fill your days?"

"I would have time for laughter. We are magic dust. Consciousness is the gift of life."

I was losing the thread of this conversation. "Can you explain?"

"Yes. Some seek pleasure, happiness, applause, meaning. No problem with that. But they miss the message: with it, all else flows."

I sighed. "Not sure I follow but is this a spiritual path?"

He nodded. "Message of all traditions. Experience sacredness: all doors open. Need nothing else. Strip away everything, you have nothing, but everything. Be in the present, but even times of distant memories and future thoughts can contain golden moments of awakening."

I agreed. "I had sacred moments during my trip, such as when observing a security guard in London and even feeling safe after being attacked by a dog. I thought that spirituality could only occur in the present. I think what you're saying is a sense of wonder could even occur as I think of spiritual moments in the past, and even the future. So maybe being in the present is key but being in other time frames could also be spiritual and sacred."

He replied, "Doctrines and absolutes are never true; Keep your mind open. Think about today being your last day on Earth. What would you do?"

"No idea, but I hope I'd find something important."

Concluding the conversation, he said: "Make every day your last. Need to catch my train. Good luck with travels."

"Okay, thanks for your time and for sharing your ideas."

The ideas seemed bizarre but some sounded right if I'd understood them correctly. Experiencing India was going to take me in new directions.

My first objective was to get to India's capital, New Delhi, where I needed to be reimbursed for the money stolen in Turkey. I had a meager $75 left. Retrieving the rest of the $400 stolen would be a game-changer and allow me to continue my travels.

Because India had once been a British colony, it made sense that many Indians spoke some English. I was told by fellow travelers that India was home to thousands of ethnic groups, tribes, castes, and religions. Hindus make up nearly 80% of India's population, with others being Muslim, Christian, Sikh, and Jain. While lower-caste Hindus ate all meat except beef, those from the higher castes, along with the Jains, were vegetarian. Farming was the largest source of employment.

Throughout the fascinating cultural and religious landscape, one issue stood front and center. The poverty was crushing and overwhelming. I was stunned to see several dead people lying on the streets, and others with limbs missing, most likely due to leprosy.

EXPERIENCING SACREDNESS: A PSYCHO-SPIRITUAL JOURNEY

As I traveled to New Delhi, our bus stopped at a traffic light, and a mother approached my window, pushed her baby toward me, and pleaded, "Give me some money or my baby will die."

My heart swelled with sorrow. I reached into my pocket and fished out a coin. I was about to hand the coin to the mother when the bus lurched forward and chugged away while spewing noxious diesel fumes. The mother chased the bus. I tossed the coin out the window in the hope she would find it. I looked back through the rear window but all I saw were plumes of dust. I was shocked and overwhelmed with sadness for her and so many others who were in this desperate life-and-death situation.

Arriving in New Delhi, I checked into an inexpensive hotel. The check-in area hadn't been swept in a long time, and the so-called mattress was an inch thick if it was that. The water from the tap was ominously brown. The weather was insanely hot and humid. Perspiration drenched my clothes, the fabric sticking to my skin.

The next morning, I woke up with red welts over my entire body. I had been bitten by bed bugs. I was so exhausted I'd slept through their attack that night while being eaten alive. The welts and itchiness grew more irritated as the day grew warmer and I perspired.

As I walked the streets, I felt like the lead actor in an insect epidemic horror film. I saw bugs in all sizes, colors, shapes, and species, and several two-inch monster cockroaches that ran across the floor. I observed locals sitting for hours picking the lice out of each other's hair. Meanwhile, amidst the deep suffering, the Jains showed their reverence for all things by wearing a cloth over their mouths so as not to kill any organisms in the air.

Indians slept in various ways, some sitting, some lying on dirty concrete floors, and some reclined on benches. Some men wore pants and others just toga-like cloth. Most Indians walked barefoot. The locals used bathrooms that were just holes in the ground, where they would squat, defecate, and when done, use water to clean themselves instead of paper tissues. Dishes were cleaned by finger-washing the plates in dirty water.

I prayed I would not get hepatitis. The stench and filth permeated my pores. I imagine that most New Delhi citizens had been smell-challenged and paid no regard to the stench. I longed for my country's conveniences when confronted with this starkly different way of life on the streets of New Delhi.

Image by Peter van der Sluijs of Poverty in India with Creative Commons

Many people spit on the pavement while their sacred cows defecated everywhere. Ah, yes, the cows...they were everywhere and oblivious to people walking by or cars driving by. When a cow decided to cross the street, traffic would come to a halt while the ever-aggressive drivers who usually drove recklessly while blaring their horns waited patiently for the cow to meander across the street.

EXPERIENCING SACREDNESS: A PSYCHO-SPIRITUAL JOURNEY

The inherent chaos of New Delhi took on another level when cows were included. Still, I was okay with that, primarily because I appreciated that most Hindus were vegetarian, and I was too. I'd read up on sacred cows before my travels. Turns out that for many Hindus, the cow in Hindu mythology is depicted as a companion to several gods, like Shiva. Nonetheless, there was a glaring dichotomy when cows were considered sacred while people starved and died in the streets.

Back to American Express

The American Express office in New Delhi was in a large colonial building and was a welcome sight. Looking forward to being reimbursed, I toyed with the idea of getting a nice hotel room for one night, possibly one with AC and a cold bath where I could soothe the bed bug bites. After all, some decadence would be fair after my trials and tribulations. I sat and waited patiently for my name to be called.

"Leonard Jason."

The first thing I noticed about the clerk was the blank expression on his face, as though he already knew we would waste one another's time. He adjusted his wire-rimmed glasses as I explained how my money had been stolen in Turkey, and how an official from American Express in Tehran had given me 100 dollars but had assured me the remaining 400 dollars would be waiting for me at the office in New Delhi.

"Who did you speak with?" he asked, barely looking up from the paper in front of him.

"I didn't get his name."

"Do you have any paperwork to indicate the loss?"

I was losing my patience. This building was supposed to be the site of my salvation, not yet another place to be questioned and denied.

"Can't you just call your office in Tehran?"

The clerk rolled his eyes. "It's against our regulations."

"Look my name up in your records. You'll see I purchased the checks in the U.S. Why would I buy the checks if I couldn't get a refund on the off chance they were stolen?"

He stared at me blankly. "I can't help."

I felt my eyes growing wider and vaguely wondered what I looked like to an outsider. Bug-eyed and desperate. "You can't do this to me."

The clerk straightened his traditional Indian clothing and looked right past me. "Next customer."

"You can't do this. I'm your customer. You can't dismiss me like this. Look at me. Look at me!"

Unphased, the clerk got up to leave the room as I felt like shouting after him.

I felt shell-shocked, crushed, and unsure of what to do. I had 70 dollars left in my pocket and I was stranded in a foreign country where I knew no one. But the shock was more than that: I had never been treated like this before. Ripped off, refused to be given the services I paid for, services I was promised. I was helpless.

I slowly walked out of the room; my eyes focused squarely on the floor in front of me.

Where did this systemic aggression come from in the human world? How could I make sense of it?

EXPERIENCING SACREDNESS: A PSYCHO-SPIRITUAL JOURNEY

As I walked back to my hotel, the locals stared at me. Their eyes were dim with poverty, sickness, and hopelessness. Many slept on the street, begged for money, and were close to dying of hunger. Once again, I questioned my 'search for spiritual meaning'.

This was the lowest moment of my trip. I asked myself whether I was trying to be a modern-day Christ, overlanding through Europe and the Middle East to reach India in my youthful quest for self-illumination. I had naively hitched through treacherous deserts where locals hungrily waited to lighten me of my material possessions as they did in Turkey. I had found myself poverty-stricken, dehydrated, intermittently sick, and traveling on an infamous stretch of history's formidable Silk Road. Now crippled without the energy and mobility I had proudly heralded until then, I was not sure how I could continue my odyssey, questing for the sacred that would deliver me. Yet, I also realized I needed to *un*learn old ways, to learn new ways of coping, to pull out the hidden potential required to surmount these unexpected encounters.

My search for religious guidance in India was now becoming a search for survival with my difficult financial situation. I decided to head to the mountains where I could rest in cooler weather. Where I was, the oppressive heat and humidity accentuated the stench and air pollution. It overrode the misery and famine with suffocation, as the air was barely breathable.

Himalayan Mountains

I headed for Manali in the Himalayan Mountains. I asked a few Indians which train I needed to get on. A helpful man showed me to the right train and fought to get me a seat on the packed railway passenger coach.

Image by archer10 of crowed Indian train with Creative Commons
Attribution-Share Alike 2.0 Generic

I traveled in third class which was as inexpensively as I could to
conserve money. The train was crowded and hot, with people sitting on
the floor, cramped together in a small space. Even though India's train
system is quite a marvel, some of the trains, built by the British, were
almost a century old and showed their wear and tear. Seat covers were
heavily stained or torn. Windows were stuck and refused to open. The
floors were sticky with who knows what. It was a cheap way to travel,
and one got what one paid for.

From 11 am to 5 pm, the train headed for Chandigarh, called the City
Beautiful. The goddess 'Chandi' gave the city its name, which also refers
to the fiery power of anger.

I noticed an older, white-bearded, well-tanned, barely dressed Indian, the type one associates with wise gurus. He seemed as if he had walked out of the jungle after a thirty-year meditation. I found a seat next to him and introduced myself as I had done with so many others over the past few weeks. We spoke about my journey and some of the people I had met. I also explained how I was somewhat discouraged, given my financial situation.

He responded, "You've been searching for wisdom and mystical experiences?"

"True."

He countered saying, "What you want, very simple, to see the beauty of creation. But friend, you have too much fire, an imbalance. Life will get hotter, more intense, and spread to find a weak spot."

"Could you explain?" I asked, not sure I understood what he was saying.

"At any moment, two paths, one fear, the other calm. What you think and experience key. If fearful you can't see what is in front of you. When content, you will have all the world's gifts."

"It's that simple?"

He responded, "We are energy. What you think and feel affects your body. If at peace, you have healing energy. If you eat right and spend days doing what is good, you can deal with anything, even disease and death."

I had to differ from him. "If you have a deadly disease, it doesn't matter what you think. You are going to die eventually, and best to try to at least get the best medical treatment."

He countered, "I have seen healing of the most serious illnesses. The body has the power to heal itself. People need to be rid of the stress that has come from living. Find a way to heal; find a way to be simple. The body can heal, but soul and brain need allow it."

I had to admit some parts of what he was saying made sense. This attitude sounded closer to psychology. I asked him, "Can we learn from the field of psychology?"

He grinned. "Emotional blockages lead to physical ones. All types of meditation eliminate grief and anger. Forgive yourself and others, bring yourself back to balance and the ability to feel gratitude."

Intrigued by this comment, I asked, "Can you tell me more?"

"Love yourself, love others, love what you are doing. That is all. Do not let demons from past interrupt present, make peace with them."

I was moved by these comments and felt compelled to open up and share my inner thoughts with him and asked, "Can I explore my past with you?"

"Of course."

"I was an awkward teenager, mediocre at best in sports. I did well in school but did not push myself. This changed when I went to college. I worked hard and almost achieved an A in every class. Maybe it was a way of seeking parental and adult approval."

My new friend said, "Dig deeper. Where are the imbalances?"

"Not sure. I guess there might have been a darker side motivating me. My culture and religion urged me to defeat evil forces. As a youth, I became a vegetarian after seeing lobsters boiled alive for our supper. I felt it was evil to kill the lobsters. But now I have seen evil on my trip, with a driver opening his car door to try and hit me and American Express refusing to reimburse my money."

"Is it evil or something else."

"What do you mean?"

"Maybe aggression is what you see, and it is a natural part of the world."

"That makes sense. I've seen a great deal of that on my trip."

"Maybe these forces are within us all."

That was a stunning realization, and I replied, "an unsettling proposition, to say the least."

"Worth more exploration." He then stood up while the train screeched to a stop. "This is my destination." He held his palms as if in prayer. "May your journey be safe and fruitful."

"Thanks," I mumbled and watched him get off the train and walk into the dilapidated train depot.

I didn't know his name or anything about him but for the next few hours, I continued thinking about his ideas. I had the fleeting thought that my hard work in school was an attempt to protect myself, to prevent something, to avoid something, but what exactly this something was I still needed to discover. I needed to also explore the issue of violence that I had seen on my trip. Was there evil in the world or was what I had seen just part of the natural world, with aspects of aggression within us all, as suggested by the holy man?

At Chandigarh, I took an all-day bus ride to Manali, a northern village that in many ways resembled Switzerland. It was in the snow-capped Himalayan Mountains of Himachal Pradesh, at the northern end of the Kullu Valley. The cool climate allowed me to escape the heat of the New Delhi plains. I was told that the Kullu Valley was also named Valley of the Gods because it has numerous pilgrimage destinations that attract worshippers of many religions, be they Buddhist, Hindu, or Sikh. The valley had wide and flowery meadows and breathtaking views of the Himalayan Mountain peaks, their ancient boulders piercing the heavens—a spiritual event indeed.

As this region was known for mountain climbing, several people on the bus invited me to go hiking with them. But feeling exhausted from the train and bus rides, I told them I needed to rest. In the center of the village, I found a hotel for two rubies a night or roughly eighteen cents, and I shared my room with another person from the states. We had something to eat, and I was slowly feeling better after the long trip from New Delhi.

My roommate was Rich, a lanky fellow from Laguna Beach California. He wore his long black hair in a ponytail. His tall and bony physique stood out amongst the local populace. People stared at him as if he'd fallen from the moon, which was ironic because the guy was stoned all the time.

"Doesn't all this weed give you a headache?" I asked.

"No. I'd have a headache if I didn't smoke weed."

"How do you know?"

"I just do, but why should you care? You do your thing and I'll do mine. Don't worry, I actually like you even if you won't get high with me."

"Much appreciated. So how do you seek happiness?"

"Me? I like cash. I call it money therapy. Ain't nothing that money can't heal."

"That's silly if you don't mind me saying."

Rich shrugged. "To you it is. My name's Rich and I plan to be rich, no, I plan to be wealthy as a motherfucker."

"And how do you plan to do that?"

Rich waved his bag of weed. "Get this shit back stateside. California hippies will eat it up."

I chuckled. "Okay, but how will you smuggle the shit back to California?"

"Fertilizer."

"What?"

"I go back to California and get funding. Next, I come back to India and buy the fertilizer and pack the weed in the fertilizer bags. That way the dogs can't smell it. I already got a connection in Delhi for fertilizer, and I know the local weed growers in this area. Bang, bang, and here comes the cash."

"I like your idea of import-export but maybe you should stick to textiles? I can see a decent profit margin and it's legal."

Rich hemmed. "That's not a bad idea."

"Thanks, so you're basically a materialistic capitalist pig?"

He saluted. "The ugly American in the flesh."

"No way, you're a stoned hippie."

He shrugged. "Why can't I be both?"

My Dad the Comedian

"You're funny, and I know humor as I grew up in an entertainment family. My dad's a comedian."

As Rich and I walked through the village, he asked me to tell him more about my upbringing in my unusual family.

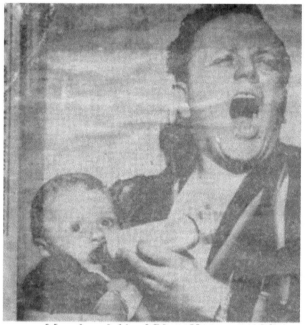

Me and my dad in a Midwest Newspaper article

"During my early years, we traveled from town to town in the Midwest. I think my escapades of running away and other rebellious behaviors, like when I climbed an unattended light fixture during my father's appearance on the Ed Sullivan show in 1952, influenced my parents to settle down in one location. We moved to River Edge, New Jersey, close enough to the Catskills mountains so my dad could drive to hotels in the evening to do his shows."

EXPERIENCING SACREDNESS: A PSYCHO-SPIRITUAL JOURNEY

Although we were now rooted in one location, our life was not typical of a middle-class family. Our family friends were entertainers, and we were surrounded by singers, comedians, jugglers, magicians, and memory experts. I remember Dave Dargan reciting phone numbers of people I had randomly selected from the Manhattan New York phone book, David Fry practicing Richard Nixon imitations, and I can still visualize the dozens of comedians, including Jackie Mason, Corbet Monica, and Don Rickles, trying out their latest comedy routines in our living room."

"Sounds like a fun childhood," Rich said.

"Yeah, it was."

As we talked, I remembered a conversation when my dad described how he became an entertainer as well as some of the entertainers he had known, including Woody Allen, Jerry Steinfeld, and Marilyn Monroe (my dad's Wikipedia page is in Appendix B). I then recounted to Rich what he had told me: "As a child, I snuck into Vaudeville shows to watch the comedians, and later appeared in several high school plays. One day, after taking a French class, I inadvertently began speaking with a French accent. Several of my friends mentioned I sounded like Maurice Chevalier, whom I had never heard of. So, I went to see one of Chevalier's motion pictures. Recognizing I could closely imitate this movie star, I bought a straw hat and started singing some of Chevalier's songs for my friends. Since this was so easy, I began imitating other movie stars at parties in high school. Soon I was doing different dialects and imitating leading entertainers of the early 1930s like Jimmy Durante.

After graduation, my family needed money, so I was a caddy during the daytime, and at night I took courses at the University of Rochester where I majored in linguistics. These were the depression years. With saloons opening up in the early 1930s after prohibition had been repealed, amateur shows with a $5 first-place prize became popular. I entered many of these contests in 1933 and often won first place. In 1934, I won $10 at the Chateau, and this led to a weekly contract at this club in Rochester. I first earned $10 a week, which soon increased to $15 a week. When I began imitating President Roosevelt, more people began coming to the club to hear me. One evening, a gambler came into the Chateau to see me perform. He said there was a gambling place outside of Buffalo, in Tonawanda, and that he could get me a job there. When he asked me how much money I was getting a week, I said $15. But the gambler thought I had said $50. So, the gambler called the owner of the club, and I got the job for $50 a week. For a teenager during the depression, this was an incredible amount of money. From here, I landed a job at the Palais Royale in Buffalo, also for $50 a week.

It was in Buffalo that I met Labe Peltz, who was a dancer from Cleveland. We became friends, and when I next played the Mayfair in Cleveland, I would stay with Labe, who it turned out was the uncle of your mom. My next job took me to Detroit, and when the manager offered me $100 a week, I couldn't believe what he said. It turned out Joe Penner was from this area, and my imitation of him was so good that they loved me. The club's owner was part of the infamous Purple Gang. I sent all the money home to my mother, and she thought I was robbing banks.

For four months in the 1930s, I joined Benny Davis, a songwriter who wrote "Margie," "Good-bye Broadway," "Baby Face," and "Carolina Moon," and he had a review called "Future Stars of Broadway." At age 19, I was doing 4 or 5 shows a day in a theatre that had vaudeville, a movie picture, and several entertainers. We played in Chicago (the Oriental theatre), Philadelphia, and other places in the Midwest. Gaining confidence, I started doing comedy with my imitations. From 1934 to 1942 (when I joined the army), I played the leading nightclubs in Cleveland, Columbus, Chicago, and Detroit.

EXPERIENCING SACREDNESS: A PSYCHO-SPIRITUAL JOURNEY

In 1937, I met Dean Martin at the Half Moon nightclub in Steubenville, Ohio. Dean was a pit boss at a gambling casino, and this was before he had his Italian nose fixed. I heard Dean sing, and he had a pleasant Bing Crosby-like voice. Dean wanted to be a singer and he approached me and asked if I might want a partner. Dean said that he could be a straight man and also sing a few songs during the act. I was not looking for a partner, and I declined this offer. Later, Dean hooked up with Jerry Lewis. The rest is history. In the late 1930s and early 1940s, I was one of the rising stars. My friends included Danny Thomas, Joey Bishop, and Sammy Davis.

From 1943 through 1946, the war years, I was in special services. I worked for the Air Transport Command band, and I was the comic with this band. I would be in the band feigning playing a trumpet, and the bandmaster would at one point ask me to come up and tell some jokes. During these years, I continued developing my comedy routines by doing shows for the troops.

There were only a small group of comedians, probably about 150 in the 1930s and 1940s, who were popular enough to work, and I was in this elite group. After World War II, I returned to Toledo where I was well known. I started dating your mom in Cleveland and we were married shortly after the war.

I met many interesting people during the war years. For example, I met Lucky Luciano (who had been prohibited from returning to the U.S.) at a café that the band was playing at in Sicily. After the show, Lucky approached me and he told me I was very funny. Lucky mentioned that after the war ended, he would make telephone calls to some of his buddies to help me get onto the radio and to play some big spots. Lucky's eyes were always shifting as he spoke to me. I had met other gangsters before the war years. For example, at one show at Jim Colisemo's place in Chicago, Ralph Capone (the brother of Al

Capone) was in the audience, and when Ralph and a friend were talking during my act, I began throwing put-down lines at him, not knowing who he was. For example, I said 'Only one fool at a time,' meaning for Capone to shut up. The band leader told me who this was, and urged me to desist if I wanted to stay alive.

After the war, I also met Issie Drucker. He had gone to a show to see his nephew Lou Bartel, and I was on the show with him. For about a year and a half, Drucker became my manager. And about 1951, he helped me get appearances on the Jackie Gleason show and Mike Wallace's program. Drucker was personally charming, but also a dangerous gangster. For example, at one benefit attended by jukebox owners, many of whom were gangsters, I was the MC. I introduced people like Harry Belafonte and Bill Haley and the Comets. The union had threatened to cancel the event because some of the entertainers were not union members. Drucker (who had organized the event) approached the union members and told them "I will break your legs," and they caved in because they didn't want to mess with this tough and rough Jewish gangster. When Drucker requested a 5-year contract, I told him that my wife would divorce me and that my rabbi had told me not to be involved with crime, so Issie let me out of his control.

I also met Meyer and Jack Lansky, who were other influential Jewish gangsters, when I entertained at the Thunderbird Hotel in Los Angeles in the mid-1950s. When the Lansky's heard that I had been connected to Drucker, they wanted to know how he was, and they remarked he was a fine gentleman. I agreed with them, but I knew that Drucker was a murderer. Later, Drucker ended up being killed.

In the late 1950s and early 1960s, I used to drive Jackie Mason up to club dates in the Catskills because Jackie didn't have a car. Jackie was at our house frequently during that time. Jackie was always on the make for women. He tended to make sexual comments about women both on and off the stage. For example, after seeing a beautiful woman, he would say: "Do you see the ass on that gal." At our house, he jokingly said to my wife, in front of me, "Do you fool around?" I always felt that Jackie was one of the funniest of the comics around. Jackie Mason received one of his big breaks from me when I recommended Jackie to replace me at the Slate Brothers nightclub in California. Steve Allen had heard of me and went to catch my show, but I had left the engagement the previous day. When Steve Allen saw Jackie Mason, who had replaced me, Steve invited Jackie to be a guest on his television show.

I would often test out jokes, monologues, imitations of actors, and new ideas in front of our family. I sing, dance, do imitations, and feel like I know about every joke written. I have the energy of a child when I am on stage. During my career, I have had the opportunity to meet many famous people. For example, one of the biggest stars on the popular Arthur Godfrey TV show was the McGuire sisters. The three McGuire sisters had hit records such as: "Sugar in the morning," and "May you Always." In the early 1960s, I worked as their opening act for four weeks at the Latino Casino in Philadelphia. The McGuire sisters liked my act as I did a great imitation of Arthur Godfrey, and I warmed up the audience for them. After the McGuire sisters finished their act, they brought me back to take a bow, and I did a few skits that they liked. I would say: "If only I could put a dress on, we could call ourselves the four McGuires." Because they had a hit song "Sugar in the Morning," I would rib the sisters by saying: "Sugar in the morning, sugar in the evening, sugar at supper time—you're going to wind up with diabetes."

The McGuire sisters later asked me to open for them at the Chez Paree in Chicago. At the end of one show, I went out to the audience to sit down with my agent, Paul Marr. At the table was a man who asked me: "Can you bring the McGuire broads over here. I would like to buy them a drink." I barked back: "What do you mean broads. They are the stars of the show. They don't mix with guests." My agent Paul then kicked me under the table with his foot and asked if he could speak privately with me. Paul told me that the person I was talking to was Sam Giancana, the biggest gangster in Chicago. I said to myself, "Oh my god, he could rub me out in a minute." I went backstage and asked the McGuire sisters if they might like to meet this famous gangster. Phyllis McGuire came back to the table with me, and Sam bought her a drink. Later, Sam approached Phyllis at the Desert Inn in Los Vegas and mentioned that he had met her in Chicago. They began dating and subsequently lived together for several years before Sam was killed. So, I guess I had something to do with bringing these two people together.

Before Woody Allen became famous in the mid to late 1960s, he had approached me and offered to write my jokes. I was in his agent's office when David Jonas introduced Woody Allen to me. David mentioned that Woody would like to work on some material for me, as he had seen me several times in the Catskills. I had heard of Woody and had seen him a few times at places such as the Blue Angels, La Reuben Bleu, and the Village Gate. Woody later submitted several monologues to me involving the theme of being uneasy about life. After looking at the material, I felt his off-beat humor would have been too wild for my audiences in the Catskills. I thought that "this skinny, little fellow" was a bit nuts, but he was also original and unusual.

On the other hand, Bob Hope would come to my nightclub performances and just watch and study me. At the Chi-Chi club in Palm Springs, in the early 60s, Bob walked up to me at one of my performances and said: "Jay, you belong." Bob had a reputation for being laconic, and I asked: "What do I belong to?" Bob then said: "You know what I mean." In show business terms, belonging meant that I belonged in the business of being a comic. This was the way one comic would complement another. Later at a supper table, I said: "I'd like to be in your next picture, and I promise not to overshadow you." Bob responded by saying: "You might." I responded: "Isn't it about time that you retired. You're an old man." Bob who was about 70 at that time began to laugh.

Buddy Hackett, I would describe as a cartoon-like figure, who talked from the corner of his mouth. Entering show business in the 1940s, he was one of the filthiest comics and often used four-letter words. I once saw him open his act by saying to a lady in the front row: "Lady, if I were to say fuck would it offend you?" The lady said "Yes," at which point Buddy replied: "Then get your fucking ass out of here because after fuck I am going to say suck, cunt, prick, balls" At this point, several audience members left, but many had come to hear this double x-rated show, and they applauded his use of this foul language. When I had first come to New York City and played at the Elegant club, Buddy and other comics came to hear about this new talent from the Midwest. Buddy at that time was just beginning to make a name for himself. I would see Buddy many times over the years in New York restaurants, and our banter might go something like this: I would say, "You are one of the funniest guys in the mountains. Why do you have to use such foul language in your act?" Buddy responded by saying: "Jay, this coming Sat. I am making $40,000 for an X-rated show. How much are you making?" I told Buddy that I might be making about $1500 over the weekend. Buddy then responded: "So you are going to tell me what to do." As the conversation began to deteriorate, but all with the intention of ribbing each other, Buddy said: "When you first came to New York, I thought you were going to be a real star—what happened?" I said: "Evidently I didn't have the qualities that you had: I never was as interesting a fucking old Jew as you." We laughed and continued to throw barbs at each other.

In the early 1950s, at the Town Casino in Buffalo, I was the comic at the nightclub. Marilyn Monroe was doing a picture at Niagara Falls. She had heard about a very funny comedian working at the Town

Casino, and Marilyn wanted to see him. Marilyn brought her entire entourage to my show. The manager of the club told me before the show that she was in the audience and he also told me not to introduce her because if she were to come up and take a bow, she would probably fall on her face (due to her being drunk). After the show, she came up to me and said, "I owe you a dance." I replied: "I'd like to go further but I'm married." I danced with her for about 8 minutes, and I held her as close as I could because I was afraid she might fall. She kept talking to me while we danced. She told me she laughed so hard at my jokes and she wanted me to explain some of the jokes to her. I responded that I had a tough time trying to understand what I was saying as well. I next joked about John and Bobby Kennedy. Everyone was watching me and Marilyn dance, and I reflected that in her state of mind, I could have done anything, but I was married and I had another show to do that night. Joe DiMaggio was in my audience that night, and I looked at him in front of my audience and joked: "I want you to autograph my balls." Joe came back after the show and Marilyn also came back to my dressing room. I introduced her to Joe, and Marilyn asked, "What do you do?" Joe just looked at her, and her manager told her he was one of the greatest ballplayers. They dated later and ultimately got married for only a year.

In 1962 I was at the Latin Quarter, where Marilyn Maxwell sang and danced. Rock Hudson came as a publicity stunt to see her, but he and Marilyn were gay. I would sit with Rock and Marilyn, and one evening I thought that someone was putting a hand on my knee. I thought it was Marilyn, but it was Rock, and I said to him "Don't go any further."

Jerry Seinfeld is a good little Jewish boy. I had followed him one night at the Raleigh Hotel in the late 1960s. He might have been about 18. He emptied the room. I went on the next night, after he bombed, and said to the audience, if you don't laugh, I will bring back that guy from last night. The audience laughed. Jerry later told me that I would only be in the mountains because "you are so good you will never be looking for anything else to do".

I also had a chance to meet many politicians and movie stars during my career. For example, I met Bobby Kennedy at a benefit for him at Madison Square Garden in the middle 1960s. My manager, Max Wolf, from the Charlie Rapp agency had put me in the show. After my performance, Bobby said to me: "How are you. Good to see you and thank you for being here tonight."

Alan Funt of Candid Camera had me on his television show in the early 1970s, with me dressed up in a karate outfit doing double talk. Alan invited me to come to California to appear on more shows, but I was unable to take him up on this offer because my wife had become ill and I needed to be close to her."

Amazed at the people my dad knew, Rich thanked me for sharing these stories.

More Varied Experiences with Seekers

The food in Manali was new to me. A typical breakfast was Noon Chai made from green tea leaves, milk, salt, and baking soda. I enjoyed walking around the village and relaxing in the quiet of the valley's mountainsides.

While sitting in a café and sipping tea, I met Alice and Jim, who were Tibetan Buddhists from the U.S.

Alice, skinny as a match with frizzy-reddish hair, was quick to the point. "I had a psychotic break last year and Jim took care of me while I was hospitalized."

"That sounds intense," I said and noticed her darting eyes.

"I also had a nervous breakdown a few years ago," Jim volunteered while nervously tapping his foot and fixating on his fingernails.

"I'm sorry," I said.

Alice replied, "Life is filled with suffering. Most people spend their lives attaining material and body pleasures."

"Agreed," I said. "We in the U.S. are a gluttonous bunch."

"We're all bound to reincarnate until we figure it out," Jim said.

"Are you sure about reincarnation?" I asked.

"Definitely."

I replied, "It sounds good because it denies the finality of death but how do you know?"

"Because reincarnation gives meaning to our struggles."

"I hear you, but truth is, I don't think anyone knows what happens when we die. For that matter, no one knows where we come from either."

Alice responded, "You're just a confused soul in a tumultuous universe. Without Buddhism, I would feel like I was drifting in a void that didn't give a hoot if I lived or died."

Jim's tapping foot went into syncopated overdrive. "I don't want to die."

"No one does," I said.

Alice continued, "Buddhism doesn't fear death. Death simply leads to rebirth. This belief in reincarnation, that a person's spirit remains close by and seeks out a new body and new life, is a comforting and important principle. Death is not the end of life, so it is not something to be feared."

"I have no right to judge anyone or anything. I'm searching too."

In an enigmatic way, Alice replied, "The infinity of nothingness becomes the infinity of something, which was created only to re-emerge with the sea of nothingness."

I said, "Some believe that meaning could be derived from trying to live life to the hilt, to love it, and fight for it until it's over."

Neither Alice nor Jim was impressed with this idea, which was fine with me.

I stood up. "Nice meeting you. I hope you seek what you find."

Alice finally smiled. "That's funny."

The next day I met two German fellows who grew pot in the mountains. They were both named Thomas and were known as The Toms. The pot field was the size of a football field and harvest was around the corner. The plants stood 12 feet tall and were laden with thick buds that smelled like skunks. The leaves glittered with what the growers called 'sugar crystals' which were a sign of high potency or high THC.

The Toms treated the plants with tender loving care. The most pressing issue, they explained, was when the plants became male or female. Only the females produced the buds while the males if allowed to live, would pollinate the females, and create seeds that grow in the flowers and ruin the smokable product. The desired outcome is sinsemilla.

"What's that mean?" I asked.

One of the Toms studiously replied, "Sinsemilla is highly potent marijuana from female plants that are specially tended and kept seedless by preventing pollination to induce a high resin content."

Tom added, "To achieve our goal, when the plants are 12 weeks old, a close inspection of the entire field is conducted daily. For if only one male survived to pollinate, the entire crop would be ruined. This all takes 3-4 hours and is adhered to religiously."

We got back to three shacks at the edge of the field where a vegetable stew was percolating over a bonfire. We sat by the fire and one of the Toms stuffed a large bong with fresh bud. They didn't know that I'd never gotten stoned, and I wasn't about to share that info. I figured it was finally time to get high and find out what the hoopla was all about.

One Tom took a massive hit and passed the bong to the other Tom who took a massive hit and next passed me the bong. I wanted to nonchalantly take a massive hit but broke out in a vicious cough that had my eyes tearing when the slightest smoke wave hit my lungs. I lay on the ground wheezing and trying to catch my breath.

"Sorry."

"That's okay, just take small hits. The effect should be the same."

I was now a bit weary. My next hit was tiny, yet I still ended up curled on the ground and searching for oxygen.

"He's hopeless," the other Tom said.

I finally got to smoke pot. Maybe it was weak weed, maybe I didn't smoke enough. I'm not sure but I didn't get high, which was a bummer because it was the only time I'd smoke weed on my journey and in my life. Yes, it's true, I had never been stoned.

Alternatively, another fellow smoking the weed got high and began to pontificate. "I only live once, that's when I'm not thinking in a Buddhist way, so as they say, what the fuck, I'm sitting on a rock in an empty deserted universe, that's except for the energy that's currently vibrating in me that makes me who I am."

"Truer words were never spoken," another fellow added. "Wherever you are is where you is."

Content at dissecting the universe to its fine particles, the two fellows high-fived.

We later went to supper in a restaurant, a spacious room with a high ceiling that had a three-winged fan whirling overhead, like in Humphrey Bogart's classic *Casablanca*.

One member of our group, a spectacled woman named Jill, was from Maharishi Mahesh Yogi's International Student Meditation Service.

Intrigued with this group, I asked her, "Can you tell me about it?"

"Sure, there are many centers in the U.S. To become an instructor, you have to meditate for at least two years and also take a three-month training course."

"Wasn't that the Maharishi who came to fame when the Beatles visited his Ashram in India?"

"Yes, and the Maharishi teaches that happiness could be attained by a repetition of a mantra-like Om. Our group offers a six-week training course at their Ashram in Rishikesh, but it cost 500 dollars."

Jill Provided me this List of Spiritual Sites

"Would like to go but I'm broke. Any other ashrams you know of?"

"I have visited another guru named Rajneesh, who preaches free sex and sees religion as a way to enjoy life."

"Are there any ashrams I could get into to try out?"

"There are hundreds of Indian ashrams," Jill went on to explain. "But ashrams are generally only open to those willing to spend a minimum of two years and also learn the local language."

She gave me names of other spiritual settings I could visit when I returned to the U.S.

The next day, I climbed a mountain and visited the Dhoongri Temple dedicated to the Goddess Hadimba, who was a figure in the epic Mahabharata. The temple had a four-tiered pagoda-shaped roof and the doorway told a story through the carved legendary figures and symbols wrapped around the doorframe.

Image by Amohan41 of Hidamba Temple Dungri with Creative Commons Attribution-Share Alike 4.0 International

Later that day I enjoyed taking a hot bath in the sulfur springs. Not only was the scent of sulfur strong and filled the air with a cleansing relaxation, but this was my first time bathing in weeks. Layers of dirt and grime washed from my skin into the heated pools. I was refreshed. After my wash, I smiled and greeted a man who was sitting alone near the temple. He was about 40, with a paunch and a heavily receding hairline. "Hi, I'm Lenny. Nice hot springs you have here."

"Indeed," he responded in polished English. "I'm here on vacation."

"Are you Hindu?"

"Yes."

"Would you mind sharing information about your religion?"

"Of course. Your western perceptions of reality are illusionary. Hinduism provides liberation from the bondage of the mind."

"Okay, but what is the goal of Hinduism?"

He raised his index finger. "To reach samadhi, a state of appreciation, with the ending of thoughts and where we can be free from desire, emotional turbulence, greed, envy, jealousness, or hostility. You see, the mystery transcends all definitions and categories. Imbalances in the nadis cause disease."

"I can see how that makes sense. What methods are used to deal with these imbalances?"

"Yoga, which involves body postures, concentration, and meditation practices."

He went on, "Hatha yoga, breathing, and body exercises make you healthy and strong. Karma yoga helps you accept your duties in life in a selfless and humanitarian way. Jnana yoga develops mental disciplines to gain a greater understanding of the higher realities of life. Bhakti yoga involves devoting your activities to attaining self-surrender and love to a divine aspect of yourself which could be in the form of a god, animal, or person. Kundalini yoga awakens a serpent-like life force within your body. Mantra yoga involves meditating on certain sounds to attain self-purification. Raja yoga allows you to become one with your higher self to stop the spontaneous workings of the mind."

EXPERIENCING SACREDNESS: A PSYCHO-SPIRITUAL JOURNEY

"Thanks for the info and they point to many ways to find the sacred."

He smiled. "Hope that this information about my religion is helpful."

"Yes, just what I wanted to learn about."

He stood up. "I must leave. It was nice to meet a young man from America. Maybe your travels will help your people reject materialism."

I watched him walk off and sat in the afternoon sun and reflected on the many commonalities between the different spiritual paths and how they attempted to achieve a state of gratitude and appreciation.

I was finally relaxing and taking time to reflect, but I needed to head back before my money ran out.

Later that day, I met John, a 30-ish, wiry traveler from Sweden who had some intriguing advice. "Think about working on a kibbutz. They're collective communities in Israel, usually several hundred or a thousand residents who live together and work in agriculture. They put whatever money is earned into a communal pool. No one can have an appliance unless they all can have it like if someone wanted a fan for their room, the motion goes to a vote, and if accepted, the kibbutz treasurer buys fans for everyone."

That got my interest. "That's cool. They buy in bulk and get a better deal."

"That's one way of thinking about it," he said. "You should give it a shot."

The kibbutz appealed to me as it sounded like a utopian option where I could take part in this egalitarian experiment at developing a community, while also earning money I desperately needed. My mind made up, I decided a kibbutz would be my destination. If only I could find a way to get to Israel.

John also shared his experience of living in an ashram for two months. "I went for the extreme discipline. We ate one meal a day of rice and vegetables and even occasionally fasted for a day. The eating days were spent in communion while the fasting days were spent alone in silence."

"That sounds intense."

"It was. I always had the option to walk away, and several times I almost did. One time I already had my bag packed when the najif, the man who ran the ashram, took me on a walk and persuaded me to stay."

"How did he do that?"

"He had me hug trees."

"Hug trees? How come?"

"He said that if a tree can stay rooted in one place for 100 years, surely I could find a way to stay rooted in the ashram program for two months."

"Wise words, so you stayed?"

"I did, and by the time I left, I knew I could've stayed another two months without a problem."

"But you left anyway?"

"Yes, and I did so with Najif's blessing."

"Cool, so when were you in Israel on a Kibbutz?"

"Two years ago."

"What did you do there?"

"I milked cows."

"Sacred cows?"

John laughed. "Not as sacred as in India. On the kibbutz, they had a system for the cows. Usually, a cow's milk production is good for about seven years. After that, her milk production isn't worth the feed and care it needs, and then the truck shows up."

"The truck?"

"Yes, and the cows knew exactly what was going to happen next."

"What do you mean?"

"They knew that whatever cow gets on the truck is never seen again."

"Where would the cow go?"

"To the slaughterhouse."

"That's messed up and why I'm vegetarian."

"Me too," John said, "so the cow selected would refuse to leave the corral and would have to be pulled and pushed by three strong men who beat her relentlessly with a wooden stick while she mooed her lungs out. Eventually, she gives up and gets on the truck. The truck would drive off and silence returned to the cowshed while life returned to normal."

"Hopefully, cows have a short memory," I said. "That's horrific."

"I'm pretty sure they have vegetarian kibbutzim too," John said. "You can research that."

"Most definitely."

Disastrous Encounter with Another Holy Man

As I walked to the bus depot, I saw a young woman walking with a large, brown, burlap sack balanced on her head; a blind man poking his way through the crowd; and two men carrying a third man off the crowded street and down an alley.

The bus depot, like all bus depots in India, was a unique cacophony of people, scents, sounds, and mayhem that seemed on the verge of collapse at any minute, yet still functioned relatively well if one was nimble and cautious. The filth was more than on most streets, maybe because the travelers knew they were leaving and didn't care if they left a mess behind, be it fruits, peels on the slippery sidewalk, or urination at the corners of buildings. Using a public restroom was highly ill-advised. Meanwhile, the air was saturated with diesel fumes emanating from 100 busses chugging at standstill or heading out from the depot. And whatever you do, don't walk close to the back of a bus. They pull away with disregard for anyone walking by.

I hoped to get an express bus to Chandigarh, from which I was going to take an overnight train to the Pakistan border, but the bus never showed.

One Indian at the station suggested I take local buses, and an elderly man helped find me the right one: a bus packed so tightly I had to stand bent over to fit among my fellow travelers. We passed several small villages, and the ride was bumpy, especially through the mountain passes—mostly barren slopes with wilting trees and an almost moon-like terrain.

During these many bus rides, I had time to reflect on my experiences and what I witnessed on my travels. I was at a crossroads. Traveling with so few resources helped clarify my questions even though I had many thoughts and mixed feelings.

EXPERIENCING SACREDNESS: A PSYCHO-SPIRITUAL JOURNEY

On my last bus, I sat beside a man wearing white robes. Rajan was in his 60s and spoke decent English. His head was shaved except for the tuft of hair on the back of his head.

"I'm a holy man," he said.

"Fair enough, so who made you holy?"

"We are all holy," and he added, "You look tired."

"I'm exhausted beyond words."

"I'm getting off soon. I live in a small village. You are welcome to spend the night and rest. A bus arrives every morning so you can continue traveling tomorrow."

My bones were rattling from hours of bumpy roads. I said, "Sounds good. I'm beat."

The town was tiny with unpaved streets. The shops had already closed for the day, so the village looked like a ghost town. I felt like I'd been parachuted into a Western movie set.

Rajan took me to a part of town where we saw a large imposing gate. He opened the cranking doors. We stood in front of a large field where about 50 people lay sleeping on short mats. The temperature was over 100 degrees, and Indian music blared from several loudspeakers.

Rajan walked me to an old barn. The wooden door creaked open, and I saw two cots covered with spider webs. We placed our bags in this moldy, dirty shed that was swarming with bugs.

Something moved under my shoe. It was a dying baby chick. The scene was one of the most repulsive I'd come across on my travels.

"We should bathe," Rajan said.

"I'll pass," and resorted to rinsing my head with cold water.

Then we had tea. I was exhausted and dizzy from the muggy heat. My eyelids weighed a ton. All I wanted was to sleep.

Rajan pulled a wooden cot out of the closet. He placed my sleeping bag on the cot and said, "We can share the cot."

I lay down to fall asleep with my feet stretched over the end of the cot's wooden frame. Rajan lay down on the opposite side and curled into a ball.

I was wondering whether I'd be able to sleep despite the pesky mosquitoes, bright lights, and blaring music when Rajan threw a shawl over us. I next felt his hand on my thigh.

I tossed off the shawl and pushed his hand away.

I stood up. "This cot isn't comfortable. I saw another one. Let's use it."

"It's broken," Rajan said.

"That's okay, I'll figure it out."

He brought the other cot over but wanted to share my pillow.

With my voice strained with uneasiness, "You can have the pillow."

He moved his cot towards mine. I pushed it away and realized he'd patiently wait until I dozed off and continue to try to molest me. I needed to get away, but first I had to retrieve my backpack from the shed.

"I need the key to the shed. I need to get something."

"It can wait till morning."

"Actually, it can't. Can I please have the key?"

He relented.

I opened the shed, retrieved my backpack, and said, "I'm leaving."

I opened the gate and walked out to the deserted street. I felt like I was trapped in a *Twilight Zone* episode.

I stood in the deserted town trying to plan my next move when I saw a boy riding a bicycle toward a stone building. I shouted to him, "Any way of getting out of this town?"

To which he replied, "There's a train station."

He pointed the way. And as if on cue, a train horn bellowed in the direction I was walking. I ran toward the sound as the train came into view. I jumped on as it began to depart. I had no idea where the train was heading but that did not matter. I was happy to be headed away from this grimy town and the holy man.

Luckily, the train headed in the right direction toward the Pakistan border. I was able to get a connecting train to take me even closer to the border.

I got off the train four hours later and was immediately swarmed by Indians who wanted me to take their rick-shaws or cabs on the short ride to the border. Sadly, I was too broke to afford even their meager fees and opted for another bus ride.

Reflecting on India

Once at the border, I walked into a café and saw a woman sitting alone. She sat hidden in shadow, and I shifted to get a better look only to find her staring back at me with a smile.

She was dressed as a man would dress, in khaki pants and a shirt. There was a broad-brimmed hat on the table beside her.

I made my way to her table.

"Hello. Are you from the U.S. by any chance?"

She was draped over her chair, all lanky knees and elbows, and I realized she had to be at least as tall as I was. She was tan, a bit on the dusty side, and I guessed her to be a well-traveled woman in her late twenties or early thirties. Her blue-eyed gaze was direct, and she chuckled. "British, though I know you blokes think that's all pretty much the same thing?"

"Sorry, I do that all the time." I held out my hand. "I'm Leonard but call me Lenny."

Her hand was dry, her fingers long and she had a firm grip.

"Charlotte," and she smiled to show perfect white teeth, "but I'm afraid there isn't any convenient shortening for that, at least none I'd care for."

She motioned me into the chair across the table, the wariness in her eyes receding a bit.

I sat down and had a pent-up desire to share with her what I had experienced on my trip. I blurted out, "I'm from around New York City. Most of my money was stolen in Turkey, so by the time I reached India I was almost out of funds. Still, I had a fascinating trip through Turkey, Iran, Afghanistan, and Pakistan. "

"Amazing," she said and shifted in her seat to face me.

"Yeah, it felt like I was shedding layers of protection. I got pretty sick too. I saw so much disease and poverty. It was hard to see so many people suffering. Yet my experiences were awesome, and I've learned so much."

EXPERIENCING SACREDNESS: A PSYCHO-SPIRITUAL JOURNEY

"I'd love to know more," Charlotte said, "I'm going to visit friends in India but I'd never traveled to India overland as you did. Tell me about your adventures."

"Well, if you can believe it, I recently met a 'spiritual' person who tried to molest me."

"Oh, sorry to hear that."

I shared the gory details while Charlotte cupped her mouth. "Terrible, terrible to have that happen. He's sick."

"He is screwed in his head."

"You must hate him?" said Charlotte.

"I don't know much about him. I don't hate or despise him. But he's hurting others while trying to satisfy his sexual needs. Some people put themselves in leadership or spiritual positions so they can take advantage of others who have less power. Probably happens all the time, but it's different when it happens to you."

"I think he's just evil." Charlotte added.

"Maybe when I started my trip, I thought evil existed and my role was to somehow stamp it out. Now I'm not sure, and have been thinking about this the past few days."

"What do you mean?"

"Well, I was attacked by a ferocious dog earlier on my trip. Was the dog evil? I don't think so. The dog might have been mishandled or trained to be aggressive. And the supposed holy man somehow hadn't found a way to satisfy his sexual appetite by mutual consent with others."

"So, is there evil?" Charlotte asked.

"I think some people are injured and angry, and they end up hurting others. I met a person in Paris who had a decidedly morbid view of life. I don't think he was evil. He was injured and disappointed with his life. Maybe his experiences shaped him into someone who sees the world through angry and cynical eyes."

Charlotte then said, "I sometimes feel like we're no different than animals. Nothing sets us apart. The lion always attacks the weakest in the herd, those least likely or unable to defend themselves."

These Darwinian ideas slapped me across the face. I felt at times during my trip, like a gazelle culled from the herd. Maybe the people who ripped me off were also gazelles. Their aggression was not done out of spite. They did it for their betterment, to gain resources for themselves and their families, to keep their jobs, and ensure they did not fall victim to the proverbial lion.

The thought was strangely soothing to me. "Their aggression might be an adaptive response, one reinforced and rewarded by the system we are all unwillingly part of. We know why lions act with aggression. It is necessary for their survival. They obey their nature."

"I see your point," Charlotte said, "I guess evil is the wrong word."

Agreeing with Charlotte, "Evil is a religious and moral concept, and it does not consider the reasons for the violent or aggressive behavior. I guess this is one of the lessons I have learned during my trip."

Charlotte added, "How do you stay optimistic given the behavior of these people you've been meeting?"

"I'm not sure. My journey to India was to figure out my purpose, and how I might find fulfillment in life. It's easy to become bitter and upset with what happened but I'm trying to work my way through that."

EXPERIENCING SACREDNESS: A PSYCHO-SPIRITUAL JOURNEY

"Is there something or somebody you met who helped you find this way of seeing the world in a more peaceful light?"

"Yes. I met incredible people. If you can believe it, I saw a bank guard transform the boring, repetitive job of standing at a door into something of great meaning."

Charlotte nodded. "Meet any spiritual masters in India?"

"I met lots of people that were on a spiritual path, and several who had encountered obstacles. Two Buddhists had become disoriented and one experienced psychosis as she journeyed into the mysterious world of meditation and silence."

"What do you make of this?" Charlotte asked.

"What I take from this is that while the spiritual path is open to everyone, there might be even more basic work that needs to be done, like satisfying basic needs and resolving psychological issues. I'm not exactly sure what needs to be done."

"Not sure I understand."

"I'm not sure if I understand either. I met a real holy man when traveling to the mountains and even though the train was crowded and it was extremely hot, he was kind and patient and relayed things to me that I am still processing."

"Like what?"

"He was the person who challenged me to think about whether evil existed. In addition, if I understood him, he stated I needed to find a way to create balance in my life. If I don't, I won't have a good future, and the stress of life will, in the end, make me as bitter as some of the others I have met on my journey."

"But how do you find this balance?"

"I'm not sure but this spiritual man gave me some clues. I need to think more about what he told me."

"Can you give me any more details?"

"Sure, I can try. You see, I've been a bit driven, and I'm pushing myself. This trip is an example of that."

"What do you mean?"

"How many people take off to go overland to India on their own? But that has been my style for years. I take on challenging things and try to be the best. I'm just not sure what is driving me to be like this. So, I'm looking for spiritual guidance, and it is just possible that there are other things I need to figure out before the more spiritual issues can be addressed."

Charlotte shook her head. "Now I'm confused."

I chuckled. "We're in the same boat."

Then she asked, "What did the holy man say to you?"

"Something like I need to do some digging into my past, to figure out something about myself. If there was some disturbance or issues that were not resolved, that might throw me off balance and lead to stress as well. I need to figure out what about me and my past I need to explore in more detail."

"I've also had to deal with my past," Charlotte said. "I guess we all have to. My parents got divorced, and each tried to win my support and the support of my older sister."

"I'm sorry. Any idea why they didn't get along?"

A tear formed in her eye. "Mom always complained to my dad about her work, and he got tired of listening to her every evening. Guess they lost that magic or love or whatever was once there."

"Same with my parents to a certain extent, " I said. "It's hard to listen to others and be there for them."

Charlotte sniffed and nodded. "Gotta have safety in any relationship or even in a work setting. One needs to be able to express oneself and have another listen and validate experiences. Without that, there isn't much to any relationship."

"True," I said.

Charlotte continued, "Both my parents remarried though, and that has been good. The relationships with their new spouses are better. You're right. How we're brought up does affect us and trying to get a handle on this is important."

I sighed. "In my family, there also was considerable friction and many disagreements. That might be the place for me to start. My dad is a powerful figure. My relationship with him and my mom is something I need to reflect on."

"Sounds like a good plan."

"Thanks for sharing your experiences with me and they have helped," I said.

"It's me who is thankful for you telling me about your trip and what you've learned.

I'm impressed."

"Thank you, I'm just a lunatic from the states who is having the adventure of a lifetime. You know, I probably need to check and see if I can find someone at the border to get a ride from."

"Goodbye Lenny, I wish you success on the rest of your journey."

I walked by the border thinking about how I might chat with several of the drivers to see if I could get a ride when I noticed there was a hippie bus that had two levels, like the sightseeing coaches I'd seen in London.

Wearing the smile I'd been sporting my entire trip, I approached the driver and asked, "Where you headed?"

His accent was Australian. "We're about to drive through Pakistan to Kabul."

"Nice! Can I hitch?"

"Come on board, mate."

———

Chapter 5: Living in Community

―――

Headed back through the Middle East

The Australians, Beth, Thomas, and Jack, were happy to have me join them as they traveled through Pakistan in their double-decker bus. I was appreciative of their company and safe passage, as Pakistan was not a particularly safe place to travel with the ongoing war involving the secession of East Pakistan.

And so, I began my journey through Pakistan, Afghanistan, Iran, and Turkey, and eventually on to Israel, where I hoped to work on a kibbutz and potentially earn some money. I was not sure my limited funds were enough to hold out during the long trip and the return home.

Traveling through Pakistan took a day and a half, during which we tolerated the extreme heat and an endless deluge of insects from outside. Jack, Beth, and Thomas were in graduate school and told me it was not uncommon for Australian students to take gap years and summers abroad, traveling across continents. My new friends were headed for Kabul, wanting to fully immerse themselves in the culture of that Middle Eastern city.

After purchasing their double-decker bus in Australia, they converted it into sleeping quarters and outfitted a kitchen to cook meals. The bus was adorned with various kinds of décor which made our traveling vehicle quite homey. The traditional red exterior was now painted camouflage brown, which made sense and helped the vehicle become somewhat part of the traffic landscape. Still, the double-deck stood out like a sore thumb and was of great interest to the local populace every time we pulled over for a break. The Aussies were nice enough to allow groups of barefoot kids dressed in ragged clothing to roam the bus. The wide-eyed wonder on the kids' faces was a gift that kept on giving.

Beth, Thomas, and Jack were impressed that I had traveled alone, without a car, and wanted to know more about the many challenges I faced on my travels. As I began chatting with my new friends, I realized how I had been stripped of vital resources and how meeting these three Australians was a godsend. I recounted my experiences hitchhiking, which included fatigue and health problems, incessant bug bites, being robbed, and the holy man who tried to molest me.

After hearing these stories, Jack asked, "Have you still maintained the resilience to continue your search for spiritual answers?"

"Yes, I am continuing my search for wisdom."

Thomas asked, "Did you meet any holy men in India that impressed you?"

"Several, and one guided me to insightful thoughts about balance, gratitude, and forgiveness. My physical journey was in the external world, where I had been seeking answers from others, but this guru helped shift my attention to an internal exploration."

"What do you mean?"

"I guess I need to examine issues in my past, and potential causes for internal imbalances. During my journey home, I hope to devote more time to this psychological introspection."

Probing Family Influences

Beth was studying engineering while also working towards a medical degree. She had a strong interest in family histories. Sitting in the back of the bus, with a window cracked open to let a breeze in, I asked her about her ancestors and their reason for making Australia their home.

Beth replied, "My ancestors arrived in Australia from Britain due to being incarcerated over relatively petty crimes."

"When did this happen and how many others were brought to Australia?" I asked.

"From the late 1700s to the mid-1800s, over 150,000 convicts were transported to penal colonies in Australia. When the British government sent their criminals to Australia, over one million indigenous people were dispossessed, and the consequences of this tragedy continue to have a powerful effect on all Australians."

"So sorry to hear about that. We have a terrible problem in the U.S. where Black people were kidnapped from Africa and made slaves, and they continue to be poorly treated."

Beth replied: "Every country has its sins that need to be recognized."

"Agree completely."

Beth brought the conversation back to my travels and search for what might make me happy and fulfilled. "Can you tell me about some of the holy men you met?"

"One asked me to explore what might have caused possible imbalances in my life. I am now reflecting on my family and how I grew up. I know none of our families are perfect, but our personalities, strengths, and weaknesses are developed from their influence during our formative years. I need to find time to examine how my family affected me."

Being an interested listener, Beth asked, "Maybe what happened in your past can provide you some clues to the potential imbalances you seek to uncover. Tell me about your family and where they came from before immigrating to the U.S.?"

"My roots go back to eastern Europe and Russia." (Appendix C provides more details)

Beth asked, "How did your dad meet your mom, and how was their relationship?"

"When my father was nineteen, he played nightclubs in Cleveland, and he was staying with my mother's uncle. When my dad came to Cleveland for an engagement, my mom's family came in to see the show. When my mom met my dad, she was attracted to his charisma and outgoing manner."

"There was chemistry from the start," Beth added.

"After World War II, my mother was in her early twenties, and she fell in love with my dad, who was entertaining in Cleveland again."

"What was it that your parents were looking for in each other?"

I had not thought about that before, and after reflecting on this question, I responded, "Maybe my dad saw the large home of my mom's parents, and he was impressed with their social status. My mom's dad was a successful businessman, having pioneered a 24-hour supermarket and other innovations. And I remembered he once told me, with this family background, my mom could pass on excellent genes to her children."

"Cool, your dad was thinking about his offspring right from the start," Beth replied.

My Dad and Mom

"I guess there was also a strong attraction from my mom because she saw my dad's loyalty to his family. Before marrying, he sent almost all the money he earned to his mother. I think my mom also liked his thriftiness, which was so different from her parents."

Beth clapped twice. "Sounds like a perfect match."

"Not really. My dad's mom was also bright and head of a large family, but she ended up domineering my dad."

Beth asked, "What do you mean?

"Whenever my dad's mother asked him to do something he did it, and this angered my mother. My mother felt alienated because my dad put his own mother's wishes before hers."

"Can you give me an example?"

"Sure, my dad's mother asked to have her husband live with our family. So for twelve years, my dad's father lived with our family. It made no difference whether my mom wanted him in the house because my dad would always follow his mother's wishes."

Contemplating this conflict, Beth replied, "When family decisions are made without input, I'm sure this can create friction in a family."

"That must be true, and I guess this is where our ancestors can unintentionally affect us. It is easy to see how the injustices of slavery have afflicted the Black people in my country. Our past can have devastating consequences."

Beth replied, "Wow that's heavy but so right, and please tell me more."

"My parents' relationship must have had a huge influence on me, but their parents also influenced them, and so it goes from one generation to another."

Beth asked, "Could it be that your ancestors' interpersonal problems have been passed on and you are now dealing with them?"

"Very insightful. The problems that my parents deal with have a great deal to do with the parenting they received, and the expectations that they had about what they might get from their relationship."

Beth gave me the thumbs up, "You got it; keep going."

"OK, my dad's intergenerational anger had been passed on."

Beth asked, "From who?"

"Let me think, it must have been his grandfather and mother, who he was closest to. They both had anger issues and they would explode when frustrated or upset."

Beth said, "Now we're getting somewhere."

"This is scary. Not only did it affect his relationship with my mom, but these seeds of aggression might be within me."

"Do you feel you have aggression within you that you need to deal with?"

"I don't know, but I think you are helping me uncover some deep-seated patterns. I don't think of myself as overly critical or hostile."

"That's good."

"But maybe there are parts of my dad in me, and that's a journey of a different sort for me to understand."

I was most grateful to Beth for helping me embark on this inner voyage and said, "Thank you so much for your helpful questions as I try to untangle this complicated history."

There was plenty of ground to cover through Pakistan. I now had time to think about how my trip to India started as an attempt to find what might bring me happiness. But this journey now included a psychological perspective, particularly how my parents had shaped and affected me through their relationship.

We finally passed the Afghanistan border without any trouble and next headed to Kabul, where I parted ways with the three Australians and their bus, waving goodbye to them as they drove into the city center.

Back Through Afghanistan and Iran

I next traveled thirty hours by bus through the desert until the bus broke down, and we waited until three in the morning for another bus to arrive. Unfortunately, the next bus was half the size of the first, and all the passengers were squeezed into this tightly packed bus.

A heated argument arose when a merchant carrying two cages stuffed with chickens found it reasonable for the cages to be propped on a seat while an elderly and frail woman held onto a wooden pole for dear life. The argument was settled when a burly man tossed the cages to the floor and motioned the woman to sit on them. The chickens seemed to enjoy the relative privacy provided by the woman's heavy dress. They stopped their nervous cluck, which went a long way to calm the travelers' frayed nerves.

Throughout the challenging times I'd faced, I kept reverting to the song "Smile", sung by Nat King Cole: "Smile though your heart is aching. Smile even though it's breaking. When there are clouds in the sky, you'll get by if you just smile."

I'd mumble the lyrics under my breath and rejuvenate my positive attitude. Whining never gets anyone anywhere except maybe to worse outcomes. I also found out later in life that the instrumental was written by none other than Charlie Chaplin, which makes perfect sense.

The next day, I arrived in Herat, and took another bus to Taibad, across the border with Iran. Next, I traveled to Mashhad where I took a night train to Teheran.

I continued to meet many interesting people, and my outward style of smiling and greeting people with openness was paying off. Not only was

EXPERIENCING SACREDNESS: A PSYCHO-SPIRITUAL JOURNEY

I continuing to learn about other cultures, but I also was able to travel inexpensively and conserve my limited funds.

In Teheran, I was fortunate to meet three Frenchmen at a hostel who had a car, and they gave me a ride to the Turkish border. As Frenchmen are, and as I'd experienced while traveling in France, they were nice enough if a bit stand-offish. One of the men, a tall skinny fellow with a Roman nose, spoke but a tiny bit of English. His friend, a short and stocky bloke with a well-trimmed beard, was snorting snuff and sneezing his way through the trip, blowing his nose and mumbling profanities. This habit didn't appear to bother his compatriots. Even though they were a bit rough around the edges concerning their social etiquette, they'd nonetheless offered me a ride, which was truly appreciated.

When we finally got near Turkey's border, the Frenchmen's car engine overheated and broke down so I walked to the border and crossed into Turkey.

That night I slept outside and had breakfast at a restaurant that serviced international travelers. Like many Turkish restaurants, the ceiling was low and anyone over 5 feet 8 inches needed to slouch their way to the table, shoulders tucked in. The benches were cheap, unvarnished wood, and the tables were made of metal strewn with stains. The air was heavy with the scent of spices. I introduced myself to the group sitting at a table and told them about my travels to India and some of the experiences I had. Oscar, a person from Denmark who had studied Persian for three years in Iran, overheard my experiences and mentioned the country's repressive society, and indicated he also had interests in the occult.

I asked him, "Can you offer any information about your interests in the occult arts?"

"Sure, let's try an exercise. Close your eyes. Imagine two sides of the brain, with an alley between them. On each side, there are doors with labels above the doorframes. Select one door and go into that room."

I visualized three doors on the left hemisphere labeled: fear, desire, and ego. The doors on the right hemisphere were labeled: patience, balance, and love. I entered the room labeled patience and I saw a large hole in the pavement. I would have to fall into that hole, below the realm of ordinary life, and abandon all my current attachments. I was not exactly sure what this meant but it might have been similar to the advice several of the holy men had given me in India.

I opened my eyes and Oscar said, "Let's try another exercise. Imagine what your parents might look like if you were to see them when they were young."

I saw my dad as a large, black, walrus-like animal, sitting in a small chair, and my mother as a tiny figure in white beside him. Again, not sure what these figures represented, but I thought it was an interesting exercise.

The two imaginary situations made me realize again that how I felt and processed the world in my unconscious was connected with the relationship between my powerful dad and my mother who exemplified a subservient position.

Another person at our table was from Spain and spoke with a booming voice that this was all nonsense. "What you are doing traveling around the Middle East? Start dancing; have fun. Why are you wearing that hat? I know, you are afraid of the world. Get yourself a woman and put your hand on her tit. That is the way to enlightenment."

Another person at our table, a tall, red-bearded man from a Scandinavian country, replied, "You need to see my guru. His yoga is what you need. Want to get wisdom, go to him immediately. You can't get wisdom on your own. You need my guru. He'll help you. Remember women love spiritual men."

I felt I was in a comedy movie but was feeling more and more uncomfortable with their brash comments. I was not sure if they were serious or not, but the juxtaposition of religious searching and sex was a dangerous combination, and I had just recently experienced this inappropriate crossing of boundaries in India. As the conversation grew too sexist for my liking, I parted ways with the group and continued my efforts at hitching.

A Ride Through Turkey

After waiting four hours at the border, I chatted with several Australians who mentioned they were headed to Erzurum, in eastern Turkey. The Australians, all in their late thirties, had a van that was quite full, but I hoped they might offer me a ride. At lunch, I described how my money had been stolen and how I had been subsisting on very little.

"You look like one stripe on the pajamas, mate," one of them said.

Another joined in, "Yeah, you'll have to visit Australia and we'll throw one on the barbie for you."

"What's a barbie," I asked.

"A barbecue, mate."

"Australia sounds great," I said. "Definitely something to consider if not for strictly spiritual quests."

"Yeah," the first one replied. "You visit our country for the booze, the food, the beach, and the women. Search for God somewhere else, you're not gonna find him in Australia. We're a hedonistic bunch and proud of it."

After we finished eating, they seemed to enjoy my company and invited me to join them to Erzurum, which was an offer I much appreciated.

We spent the next few days traveling across Turkey. One morning, I awoke at 5 a.m. and washed and shaved next to a gas station where we had parked for the night.

While I was shaving, the friendly attendant asked, "Can I borrow your razor?"

My impulse was to say no, that sharing a razor is almost as bad as sharing a toothbrush, but the chap had warm and kind eyes. I sensed that the shave was important for his image—he'll be spending long hours at the gas station, cooped up in a stuffy room.

I handed him the razor. "You can keep it."

"Thank you," and he reached into his shirt pocket and gave me a pen, which was fortuitous since the pen I'd bought in Geneva had just run out of ink.

The roads through Turkey were often no more than dirt paths, and I was surprised to see so many mountains with snow at their peaks. Unfortunately, the Turkish people did not drive carefully as there were many over-turned cars and buses on the sides of the roads. When we stopped the van in several towns, the locals offered us free apricots and fresh-baked bread, as they were not used to seeing foreigners.

At one stop, I noticed a young woman selling apples. She was surrounded by three young children and was holding on to a crying baby. Her back was bent like she carried the weight of the world on her slender shoulders. I tried to strike up a conversation, but she spoke no

English. She couldn't have been older than 18-20. I wished I had $100 to give her but all I had left in my pocket were pennies. My poverty was temporary. Hers was lifelong and harsh...so much poverty...too much....

I had been sleeping outside the van, and one morning awoke with only the use of one eye, and my bulging lip hanging from my mouth. My swollen face had grown puffy once again from several insect bites that had occurred overnight. Though I looked like a monster, I found it all amusing, especially as I considered all I had dealt with already on my travels.

My fellow travelers were shocked but also amused at my appearance.

"Not a good time to take a photo you want to send to your family," one said.

"I'm not sure," another humorously added. "I find him handsome in a Quasimodo kind of way, and as you know, the hunchback ends up getting the girl."

"You're a riot," I mimicked Jackie Gleason's raised fist in the Honeymooners. "To the moon, Alice, to the moon."

We continued on our way. I spent most of the time looking out the window at the gorgeous terrain and mountains.

My Australian friends had told me they had heard a port in Mersin had a ferry to Cyprus, and from there I could find further transportation to Israel. They commented it would be the only way of getting into Israel, as going from Lebanon or Syria into Israel would not be possible due to tension between the Islamic countries and Israel.

As we got close to the coast, I thanked my Australian friends and took a Turkish bus to Mersin, Turkey's largest seaport on its southern coast. The port is by ruins of the old Roman defensive walls called Cleopatra's

Gate. This was the territory where Paul had ministered, converting Jews and gentiles to the new Christian religion over two thousand years ago. It was also near a Christian pilgrimage destination called St. Paul's Well, the saint's birthplace. The beautiful scenery was truly everywhere.

That evening, I spotted a German car and walked over and spoke with the Germans for an hour as we talked about some of our mutual travels over the past few weeks.

"Have you ever smoked opium?" one of the Germans asked.

"No, it's not for me."

"It can become a bad habit but worth one try."

"I'll pass."

"I spent two days at an opium den in Calcutta. I went with a friend who knew the opium dealers and who respected him, so I felt safe. The high is so relaxing like you're walking in a meadow with God by your side."

"That sounds spiritual."

"It was for me, but only for two days. Then I walked away. Lots of addicts in India. Life is so difficult and they just want to escape to a peaceful place."

"I can for sure understand that need," I added. "The crushing poverty never ceased to affect me, no getting used to that."

"Amen."

After that, I talked to a local person who told me there were no boats out of Mersin to Cyprus. I was disappointed to learn this and thought I would need to take a bus to another port.

EXPERIENCING SACREDNESS: A PSYCHO-SPIRITUAL JOURNEY

I checked into an inexpensive hotel and had a good night's sleep. The next morning, I poked into my shoes, a precaution I had maintained to ward against finding assorted unpleasantness in my apparel, and to my surprise, a furry animal scrambled to the toe of my boot. Taken back, I hit the shoe, heel first, onto the floor and watched some type of rodent, red in color, scramble away.

In my effort to find a boat to Cyprus, I met a Turkish man who helped me find the tourist information center. I was delighted to be informed that two boats sailed to Cyprus each week from the docks at Mersin, and one would be departing that day at 5 pm. I was directed to a bus station, where a bus took me to the ferry leaving for Cyprus.

Ferrying to Cyprus

Luckily, I got to the port and bought my ferry ticket just in time. The boat trip cost thirteen dollars so now I only had forty-five dollars left to get to Israel. I hoped this would be enough. After boarding the ferry, I hung around several travelers from the U.S., Britain, Holland, and Belgium. We had lively conversations and a great deal of fun swapping stories of our various adventures.

The Belgian, a boisterous fellow with a thick beard, started by saying, "We each tell the worst thing that happened to us on our travels." He pointed to the Dutchman, a short and wiry lad. "You go first."

"Okay. I was in Manilla. If you think Bangkok is tough, you ain't seen nothing till you go to Manilla. So, I meet this girl at a bar, she's nice and speaks English, so we have a few drinks and she invites me to her place. I was drunk and she was pretty so I was thinking it'll be fun. So, we get to her place and we start having fun when there's a bang on the door and, this Filipino man walks in and starts yelling in Tagalog. The girl yells back. I'm naked at the edge of the bed. The man takes out a switchblade and points it at me. Fortunately, the apartment was on the first floor. I jump out of the window and find myself running naked down the street. I was lucky it was late at night. I hid in an alley where I found dirty rags I could wrap around my body. I lost my clothes, wallet, and shoes. I was lucky that my passport was in the hotel safe."

The Belgian clapped. "Good one, now you," and pointed to me.

I shared my encounter with the 'holy man' who tried to molest me. The travelers jeered in contempt and the Belgian replied, "That's a good one," and next pointed to the British guy. "What about you?"

"I was in Japan, which is a clean and relatively prosperous country. I met a local who invited me to a party that was to take place in an industrial warehouse on the outskirts of Tokyo. I was instructed to go to the back of the warehouse and take the service elevator to the third floor. It was dark and my friend hadn't arrived yet, so I decided to wait for him upstairs. Why? Because I'm an idiot. The elevator got stuck. I figured my friend or other revelers would show up but it turned out the party was canceled. I was stuck in pitch darkness with little air for 14 hours. I kept banging on the walls every few minutes and was finally rescued by a delivery truck driver. Since then, I can't ride in an elevator or an airplane. I can't even sit in a room with no windows."

The silence was deafening as even the boisterous Belgian was at a loss for words.

The next day, our ferry arrived at Famagusta, an old walled city in Cyprus. I ate a small snack and went for a swim. The water was warm and clean but as with all beautiful beaches, this one was also unfortunately too crowded for my liking. Still, I enjoyed my swim and felt clean for the first time since the hot springs in the Himalayas.

EXPERIENCING SACREDNESS: A PSYCHO-SPIRITUAL JOURNEY

I soon learned a plane to Israel would cost a mere thirteen dollars, so I hitched to the airport in Nicosia, the capital of both the Greek and Turkish sections of Cyprus. Nicosia was in the center of the island, in a country with a rich but troubled history. Due to fighting between Greece and Turkey between 1963 and 1964, the Greek and Turkish Cypriot communities separated into the north and south parts of the city.

Nicosia had the feeling of a quaint town. As I wandered around, I was in great spirits and saw beautiful handicrafts and folk art on sale, including well-regarded Cypriot lacework and silversmithing. I smiled and greeted many people, one being a heavy-set and patriotic American named Joe who gave me 10 bucks after I told him the story of my stolen traveler's checks.

Joe huffed, "I'd cut that clerk's balls off." With a lingering longing in his voice, he added, "This shit never happens back home."

"I guess not," and I decided to spare my criticism of other manifestations of American greed. Joe wouldn't have taken kindly to that.

"Can I have your address? I'll mail you the cash once I get back home."

"No need," Joe replied with a friendly shoulder smack. "It's my pleasure, and besides, I got more money than I know what to do with."

I was going to suggest several ways for him to 'constructively spend his money' but that would have been rude, so I smiled.

A Cypriot at a bar restaurant also treated me to free food, where I was offered Turkish coffee. The bold bitter taste was delicious.

I also met Anna, an enchanting Israeli sociology professor, and we talked over lunch.

Image of Nicosia Cyprus by Brian Harrington Spier under Creative Commons Attribution-Share Alike 2.0 Generic

"Israel is a social mess," Anna stated, "and for good reason. When you have Jews (and some pretending to be Jews) from 70 countries converging on a small parcel of land upon which already lives another people, the Palestinians, you're bound to run into trouble. Also, it doesn't help that many of the arriving migrants have suffered greatly in their ancestral lands and are traumatized, to begin with."

"Add to that the caldron of three major religions crossing paths over one city, Jerusalem, and what can you expect," I added.

"Exactly," she replied. "So now we have the Sephardim hating the Ashkenazi (and vice versa), the Arabs hating the Jews (and vice versa), the secular hating the religious (and vice versa), and everyone trying to make a few shekels at the expense of the others."

"A mess of biblical proportions," I said. "What's the solution?"

"There's no ultimate solution," Anna concluded. "It's more crisis management, like a chronic disease that needs to be monitored. One needs to accept the chaotic overtones of Israeli society as an inevitable situation. Still, that doesn't mean the Israeli experiment is doomed to fail."

"Good to know."

"Think about the Israeli collective as you would about an abused child. We carry lots of pain and trauma and end up inflicting some of that trauma on each other."

Anna and I sat in contemplative silence.

That evening I slept in a deserted room at the airport, and the clean, air-conditioned building was a true luxury. I was so relieved and happy to have enough money to travel to Israel.

Life on a Kibbutz

The next day, my plane landed at an airport outside of Tel Aviv, Israel. That night, I was kicked out of several places where I tried to sleep, so I bedded down on the beach.

When I awoke, with waves pounding the shore, I saw a deserted beach strewn with plastic wrappers and sand stained with blotchy black oil that stuck to my feet and wouldn't wash off. I took a swim in the warm, deserted waters. Although polluted, I still appreciated swimming in the historical Mediterranean, where thousands of sunken ships filled with lost treasures lay beneath the sand. In the background, Tel Aviv was coming to life with the sputtering of diesel busses and the faithful who walked down to the sea and stood in prayer.

I tried to hitch later that day but when this proved unsuccessful, I took an inexpensive bus to Tel Aviv, which is in central Israel, on the Mediterranean coastline. For thousands of years, Tel Aviv has served as a historic connection between Europe, Asia, and Africa. Although the city was a hub of economic activity and ethnically diverse, I noticed considerable urban decay.

I was delighted to learn a Kibbutz by the Sea of Galilee would pay me to work. At this point, I only had twenty-seven dollars left to my name.

I hitched out of the city and met Israelis who were assertive, even a touch arrogant, and yet also proud and courageous. I admired their fierce spirit. Hitching was not easy in the hot Israeli climate, and I could feel the sun's rays penetrating my skin. I hitched north, up the coast, the dunes and sea to my left, orchards laden with oranges to my right, and headed into the lower Galilee valley where the fertile land was covered with a blanket of colorful fields. The flush of a warm sunburn heated my body.

Finally, after a day's travel, I descended from the higher Galilee to flat land and a large lake known in Hebrew as The Kinneret (the Sea of Galilee). A bit south of there, I arrived at Kibbutz HaOn, in the Jordan Valley. This was a utopia, with palm and date trees across the property, and wild exotic flowers blooming. Established in 1949, this kibbutz had many confrontations with Syrians at the close Golan Heights border. Israelis still walked around the kibbutz with machine guns for protection in case of another confrontation.

Volunteers were provided clean rooms and cabins and even a private beach. The austere cabins were more like wooden shacks with thin walls. You could easily hear a conversation from the adjacent room. The floors were concrete, and the rooms were small with four single beds per room, a small closet without doors, and a rickety wooden desk and clunky metal chair overlooking the yard through a curtainless window.

EXPERIENCING SACREDNESS: A PSYCHO-SPIRITUAL JOURNEY

The one-story building also had a bathroom/shower that was shared by the volunteers.

On my first day, I was assigned to work on the banana crops. I woke at 4 a.m. and observed the dark terrain gradually change into grey dawn and later the sky turned blue. At breakfast, I had biscuits and coffee with Emilie, a volunteer from Finland. After eating we were off to the fields. With a scythe in hand, my job was to cut the dead branches off the green ten-foot banana plants. Flies, mosquitoes, spiders, and snakes infested the area. I wondered if I would be able to survive the first day, but I kept chopping and chopping at the dead leaves, trying to keep up with the others. The leaves were constantly in my face as I was bending and stooping to pull off the dead bark at the bottom of the banana plants. The pace of the workers was quick and methodical. I pushed myself and kept the mantra "I can do it" playing in my head, but I felt there was no way I could keep up with everyone else despite my efforts. Finally, we took a break, and I was able to rest. Fortunately, we had many breaks, and this enabled me to keep up my energy for chopping and I became a bit more efficient over time.

Over the next few weeks, we had the same routine, being awakened at 4 a.m. by an Israeli with a machine gun coming into our dormitory room and shouting in Hebrew "Boker Tov" or good morning in English. At 8 a.m. we had breakfast in a communal air-conditioned cafeteria: tomatoes, milk, cheese, yogurt, eggs, bread, and jam, a spread fit for a king. We returned to the fields at 9 a.m. With the sun blazing by noon, our workday was over, and we had lunch, where I stuffed myself, and would then take a much-deserved nap. My hands often hurt as they were becoming calloused.

There was plenty to do and many different types of work, but all typically included hard labor. For a few days, we were assigned to work on the date trees, and we put mosquito nets over the treetops to protect the fruit. We climbed extremely tall ladders to get to the proper height. One volunteer even fell from a ten-foot height and was taken back to the cabins to rest.

We also worked several days on irrigation and watering fields while other days were spent harvesting the grape fields. We were sometimes tasked with collecting discarded tools for the kibbutz along with a bit of gardening. One of my roommates got a hernia from the work; he was operated on the following week. The volunteers often walked around with bandages on their hands, as many accidents occurred daily.

A scorpion was killed outside my room where I had been previously walking around barefoot. One day, I was lifting a concrete divider from a barren field when a monster spider crawled out from beneath the divider. The size and shape of this creature were straight from a horror movie.

The scariest possibility though was the poisonous snakes, which kill more humans every year than any other animal. These poisonous vipers at my kibbutz had a unique zig-zag design on their backs. If a venomous bite was not treated within two to three hours, the person would surely die, but fortunately, there was a hospital ten minutes away. These snakes preferred the banana trees, and we thought the kibbutzniks were kidding us about their presence until I practically put my hand on one that had planted itself in a tree. The dense vegetation created a jungle where a snake could hide or rest wherever it liked, and this was what scared me the most.

In the afternoon, I showered, washed my clothes, and would go swimming or socialize with the other volunteers from the U.S., France, Italy, the Netherlands, Germany, Canada, and Finland. The volunteers talked and learned about each other's cultures. We sat on the lawn in the afternoons and evenings, where we listened to music, talked, danced, read, and joked around. I was slowly getting to know Emilie, who I began to spend more time with. Overall, the volunteers created our little community together.

Hash was always present and quite a few partook. Turns out that Israel has some great hash available via its Arab populace. The 'dealer' was Georgiou, an energetic Italian volunteer who took a weekly bus ride to Tiberius, a small city on the Sea of Galilee, where he met with Ahmed, a local fisherman who had a side business selling hash that came from Syria, across the border but a mile away. The hash was reddish-blonde, soft, and fragrant, easily as good and possibly better than the Afghan hash. I wouldn't know as I opted to stay sober, but judging by the glassy eyes and wide smiles, the hash did its job and then some. No one on the kibbutz seemed to care as long as we, the lowly volunteers, kept to ourselves and showed up to work the next day.

Certificate for working on the Kibbutz

It was also the time I met Tim, a Canadian who played the guitar like it's supposed to be played. We'd sit on the grass at night, and he'd take requests. He knew tons of songs—Beatles and Rolling Stones, The Mamas and Papas, and Simon and Garfunkel. He also had a decent voice. He had me pondering why I never gravitated to playing the guitar. The joy seemed apparent and infectious. He'd be joined by Frank, a Dutch guy who played the bongos. The sweet memory of jangling music and hash wafting through the warm air remains with me.

This experience was much more relaxed compared to my previous grueling weeks of travel. After several weeks of this Kibbutz life, I had gotten tan, was stronger, had regained the weight I had lost, and was back to my usual 150 pounds, gaining almost twenty-five pounds. I was feeling more like myself again – rebuilt from the experiences of my life on the road.

One kibbutznik I met was named Amos. He was a 23-year-old who'd recently returned to the kibbutz after completing his service in the Israeli army where he was a medic. He was planning to attend medical school, so we had some academic goals in common. He also spoke good English, which enabled us to get beyond the peripherals.

One night, we sat in the dining room and talked over a bowl of chicken noodle soup.

"If you don't mind me saying, us volunteers find the kibbutz people pretty narrow-minded and arrogant, present company excluded."

"We're like the cactus tree," Amos replied, "thorny on the outside but our fruit is sweet and juicy."

"I find the analogy wanting," I said. "The volunteers do all the dirty work, and the kibbutz people are kinda lazy, trying to get by on minimum effort."

Amos looked stern. "That's a bit harsh. "Look around you. We have a beautiful community."

"It's nice for sure but why are you guys so dismissive, like you know everything and us volunteers are a bunch of losers?"

"We're insular," he added. "Think about it. We have 200-300 volunteers come through every year, sometimes more. You guys come and go. We don't have the desire to get to know you, though we do have two couples who met and married."

"That's two out of thousands," I said.

Amos shrugged. "You don't like it, you can leave. We couldn't give a damn if you did."

"That's not a nice thing to say."

"I'm sorry but it's true. I think your expectations are too high. It's not like you're offering to stay and become a member. If you did that, maybe we'd treat you differently, knowing you want to belong, but you don't. You're going back to America where you belong."

The stark honesty in his words was indicative of what I felt: the volunteers were like passing ships in the night.

His voice softened. "Us Jews have been kicked around for centuries, pogroms, holocausts, religious persecution. We were weak and powerless. We're not anymore. We have a country, we have an army, and we have our national pride. We're a new country barely 25 years old. We're learning how to become a family. It's hard. Jews come from all over the world. Jews argue about everything all the time. The kibbutz is where we finally feel safe, where we can tell the rest of the world to fuck off."

I liked Amos. He was intelligent and articulate but carried the same arrogant trait that I found offensive. Maybe the problem was mine. I was too soft and had too many humane expectations. The guy just got out of the army where he was taught to kill Arabs without a second thought. The kibbutz people had blind hatred for Arabs. I understood the historical links but was perturbed by how one collective hates another collective without any issue. The Arabs want to kill the Jews for taking their land, and the Jews feel the land was righteously given to them by God since the days of Moses. Once again, more violence is being passed down from generation to generation, and it reminded me of my conversations earlier with Beth in Pakistan.

Before the 1967 six-day war, Syria was within shouting distance of the Golan Heights. The kibbutzniks had banded together for twenty years in defense of their country. Now with fewer terrorists in the area, and the danger of annihilation diminished, the kibbutzniks had become complacent. The kibbutz was wealthy but lacked a sense of community between the volunteers and the kibbutzniks. I did not see any spirit of brotherhood and love. Their double houses were air-conditioned, with TVs blaring at night. A few of the best families were leaving the kibbutz. I had journeyed to this kibbutz with the hope of finding an egalitarian community, but I did not find what I had imagined. I hoped there were other kibbutzim able to maintain the vital communal spirit I had hoped to find. Later, I would learn in 2007 that, due to debts, this kibbutz would have to sell its businesses and return its land to the state of Israel.

I asked several kibbutzniks if they knew anyone with a deep knowledge of the Jewish religion and if any of these aspects involved mysticism. They introduced me to Jacob who lived at another kibbutz. We met one afternoon.

I shared with him where I had traveled and what I had seen along the way, ultimately leading me to the kibbutz.

He then offered this insight, "You can find all that you are looking for in Judaism. Our religion has a stronger social ethic than the other religions you have encountered."

"Can you tell me more?"

"Sure, the Torah is clear in prohibiting injustices. Rather than a loss of identity as practiced in several of the eastern religions, Jewish mysticism, or the Kabbalah, has a relationship between you and God, and the Messiah will one day restore the world to a state of harmony and flow of divine love."

"Sounds good. Can you tell me about the Kabbalah?"

"Okay. The German school is called Practical, where through prayer and meditation one tries to cultivate a constant sense of God's presence. You would probably be more interested in the speculative form from the Provence-Spanish school where the aim is to discover the hidden mysteries contained in the Old Testament, ultimately revealing a hidden meaning within every word of the narratives. The person praying experiences peace and joy, as love occurs in divine unity. Through study and prayer, we can speed up the return of the Messiah. In a sense, God's light is infused into everything, and distractions disguised as confusions hide these divine sparks from the non-believer."

"That's not that far removed from Buddhism," I said. "What practices allow someone to have this special relationship with God?"

"Hasidic traditions focus on reciting wordless melodies, visualizing the name of God, conversing with God to quiet the mind and to let in the voice of God."

"Kinda like the Buddhists do when reciting a mantra." This was a revelation, that even within my religion, there was a mystical tradition, one which could help me redefine my relationship with the divine.

More Psychological Digging with Emilie

My friend Emilie and I were spending more time together. Her parents had been in a concentration camp during World War II and most of their family had been exterminated. Her parents were not bitter though, and they had decided they would not let the horror of the camps destroy who they were. They remained loving and kind to everyone even during those darkest hours.

My trip over the summer fascinated her and one afternoon she asked me, "What have you learned from all these experiences?"

I thought a moment and replied, "While I started the journey with the hope to find wisdom and possibly even spiritual answers to what might make me happy and feel fulfilled, I now realize I need to better understand my upbringing and the influence of my parents."

"How so?" she asked.

"My mother and dad have strong personalities, and although they love each other, there is always considerable tension in the family."

"Why do you think that happens," asked Emilie.

"After talking with a person who had given me a ride through Pakistan, I realized that my parents had learned dysfunctional patterns from their upbringings and carried these lessons into their relationship."

Emilie asked, "Can you give me more details?"

"Sure, during my hours traveling through Afghanistan, Iran, and Turkey, I have been thinking about my dad who seemed easy to anger, and my mother often feeling neglected and having that anger directed at her."

"Sorry to hear that happened to your mom. But what was your mom looking for?"

"I'm not sure, but her dad had been a successful businessman, and I guess she wanted to be like him."

Emilie asked, "Did she try to launch a business?"

"Many. She was always trying something new. She might buy paintings or spend thousands of dollars on stocks to prove her worth. When my dad found out, he was not happy, and sometimes would get angry."

"Sounds like they were not compatible."

I added, "They love each other deeply, but something is wrong."

Emilie summed it up, "They're passionately attracted to each other, but also incapable of meeting each other's needs."

"You hit that one on the nail."

"You're going to be a psychologist, so can you try to analyze this situation," Emilie added.

"Maybe. I guess my mom identified with her high-achieving father, and yet in her life, she could only achieve through her husband, who tended to minimize her accomplishments. My dad had identified with his mother, who was bright but controlling, and he subsequently tried to control my mother, who refused to be dominated by him."

"Oh gee, sounds like a recipe for a disaster," Emily replied.

"I guess it has been, as my dad was seeing his mother in his wife; my mother was seeing her father in her husband. You're right about being incapable of meeting each other's needs. Neither would respect a weak person, but my dad could not treat my mom with respect or as an equal."

"Fascinating stuff," Emilie said, "How do you think this dynamic affected you?"

"On the surface, I had everything."

"But material wealth often does not translate to happiness. Tell me more about you and your dad?"

"He is loving and generous, and he will go out of his way to help anyone. He's the center of our family. Everyone looks up to him. He's witty, funny, and humorous. He's powerful and incredibly bright, having skipped several grades in school."

"Got it, but what about his temper. Where did that come from?"

"It must be that my dad was close to family members who tended to be controlling and critical. He respects power and must have been attracted to my mother because of her strong presence."

Emilie then pushed me a bit more, "I understand that we learn things from our parents and ancestors, but is there anything else that influenced your dad to be critical?"

"There must be other things that influenced him, and thanks for pushing me on this point."

Emilie stated, "Could being in the entertainment field affect him also?"

"Maybe. Many people in show business need to be the center of attention, and this need for attention and control can make them lose their sensitivity toward others. I guess he needs to be the center of attention, and when he is not, he does not like it."

Emilie said, "So it sounds like his show business background and his family role models influenced him to be loving and generous, but also demanding and controlling."

"That's insightful," I replied, "and I guess there has been no place for my mother's independent spirit, although she was instinctively attracted to my father's power, as she had been to her father's strength."

Emilie pushed further. "Tell me more."

"My father demanded people's attention, he demanded people look up to him and obey him. And when my mother, sister, or I, did not obey him, my dad would get angry, like a rumbling volcano."

Emilie asked, "Can you give me an example?"

"To win the love and attention of others, my father was extremely generous with dispensing favors. To be generous is wonderful, to use generosity as a tool for control is destructive."

"What are you thinking about?" Emily asked.

"Let me think. Okay, the summer after graduating high school, I asked my dad to help get me a job as a busboy in a hotel in the Catskill Mountains. This was my attempt to be more independent and self-reliant. My dad got me the job and I was able to make about a thousand dollars that summer, an accomplishment of which I was proud. The following year my dad told me that he had paid the maître d' five hundred dollars to secure the job for me. He thought there was nothing wrong with that act of generosity. I was pissed off as his generous action undermined what I was trying to accomplish that summer."

"He meant well but I am sorry to hear that. Did you ever tell your parents how you felt about the conflict that was occurring?"

"Not often but let me think. There was a day when I was in high school when I told my parents I could not take their arguing and fighting. After that, I think there was less arguing and fighting at home and my mom did become quieter."

Emilie asked, "How did that affect you and your mom?"

"I don't know. I wonder if my mother's love for me influenced her to be more silent. Could my action contribute to the beginnings of my mom's health and psychological problems?"

Emilie asked, "What happened to your mom?"

"She has had a few mental breakdowns. After hospitalizations, I just did not know how to be helpful."

"Do you think this is why you want to be a psychologist?"

"Must be, and maybe one day I can be helpful to her."

Finally, Emilie asked a penetrating question, "Do you think that searching for your purpose in life, for spiritual guidance, is somehow connected to dealing with these issues with your parents?"

Her comment struck me like a bolt of lightning. "I started this journey trying to find a way to be present and appreciate the world's gifts, but to be present, I have to acknowledge my upbringing and find ways to forgive both my parents and me."

Emilie concluded our conversation by saying, "A spiritual and psychological journey, that's what this is about, and thank you for sharing so much with me."

EXPERIENCING SACREDNESS: A PSYCHO-SPIRITUAL JOURNEY

Image by Digitout of Haon-home-sunset with Creative Commons Attribution-Share Alike 3.0 Unported

That evening, I looked into her eyes, "I wonder if people get addicted to drugs to have transcendent experiences? And I guess this can happen with other things like intimate sex. There are multiple ways to experience sacredness but some of these paths lead to destructive addictions whereas others are healthier."

Emilie laughed and nudged my shoulder. "You think too much."

"Yeah, you're right, but I often see below the surface of people's behavior and feel like I am on the plains of Africa. We are no different from what occurs in the wild. Maybe in the future, folks will look back and see us all as mentally disturbed for not seeing and being in the world differently, for not treating the world as a sacred place."

Emilie then captured the moment, "No matter how pretty nature is, I always feel better when you're with me." She held my hand and led me to the beach. We lay down on the sand and her blond hair fell over my shoulder. Neither of us spoke while we looked into each other's eyes. We spent the evening on the beach together. My loving and gifted friend was like a goddess to me during my time at the kibbutz.

Going Home

By the end of August, I had earned enough money at the kibbutz to choose between another hitchhiking excursion to London or flying. I chose flight. I took a plane from Israel to Paris and hitched to the coast where I took a ferry to England. I then hitched a ride with a British clergyman who was fascinated by my summer travels. He was short with a double chin that spilled over his tightly noosed clergy collar. He greatly reminded me of Alfred Hitchcock. His warm baritone and British accent were mesmerizing. I could easily imagine him narrating National Geographic documentaries. During our car ride, he asked me about my summer adventure.

After describing several of my adventures, I said, "I guess I've learned sometimes one needs to be lucky, to be at the right place, at the right time."

The clergyman asked, "What do you mean?"

"Now I realize many things are beyond my control and a little bit of luck is important. Many get crushed by lady luck and they get angry and bitter. I met some people like this on my travels, and in particular, a man named Jean in Paris. Life can crush anyone, and I was lucky. I now realize I don't have as much control over my life as I thought."

The clergyman asked, "You mentioned your trip was a spiritual adventure. Did you experience any religious epiphanies? Or learn anything about spirituality?"

EXPERIENCING SACREDNESS: A PSYCHO-SPIRITUAL JOURNEY

"I had been interested in Buddhism and still am. I don't disagree with their main points that life is full of suffering, often caused by being attached to material things."

"A basic Buddhist principle, but it does sound a bit austere."

"This notion continues to make sense to me, but I also feel we can love and embrace people and have experiences just like Zorba the Greek. The key is to participate with zest in the world. And even if we are at the same time attached to the outcomes, we can still be able to let them go. If this makes sense?"

The minister commented, "Sounds like some promising ways to approach life."

"I hope so. My trip started in London where I watched a security guard greeting the bank's customers. That was a moment I will never forget."

"Is there a particular reason why?"

"I guess he had a job most people would think is trivial or boring. He brought meaning into it, second by second, minute by minute, hour by hour. Being present in the moment, he was able to greet life with an appreciation for the wonder of creation."

"But how is this connected with your other spiritual experiences on this trip?"

"I think this is the aim of most mystical religious traditions. To bring to each encounter, each moment, an ability to be present and open to the vast experiences in front of us. Yet, people are often in a fog that makes this hard to see this."

The minister nodded. "Tell me more about this."

"From my readings and travels, I learned there are many ways to get to these truths. Everyone I met has been my teacher, from those who are skeptics to those who have lost their paths to those that have found a way to live with a sense of gratitude for the miracles in front of us."

"What teacher inspired you the most?" the minister asked.

"I met a holy man in India, who asked me to reach deep into myself, to explore any issues that might be the cause of my stress or tension; to figure out what thoughts were pulling me, in a sense, out of the present and into the past or the future. At least I think that is what he was saying."

The minister added, "From the little I know about psychology, I imagine there are always blocks in our unconscious and we need to deal with these to move on and achieve this desired presence you and the holy man are talking about."

"Yes, funny you should mention psychology. I will be going to graduate school in psychology when I return to the states."

"Has your journey provided you insights?"

"Yes. From this summer, I have discovered there are so many different obstacles to reaching a balanced life or being able to be present and have the gratitude I was speaking about."

"Tell me more."

"I started this journey to possibly find a guru, to find what was not complete in my life, to find what was missing. I was looking for purpose and meaning. That is all true, but over the thousands of traveling miles, I now see that this trip was as much a psychological journey."

The minister asked, "Have you found what you have been looking for?"

EXPERIENCING SACREDNESS: A PSYCHO-SPIRITUAL JOURNEY

"It is still a work in progress. My parents, who loved each other deeply, were also constantly arguing and fighting. I have been reflecting on how they were not meeting each other's needs, and when that occurs, bad things happen. In this case, my mom has been hospitalized many times."

"So sorry to hear this."

"Sometimes it is all confusing. I want to be happy. I want to be fulfilled. I want my life to have meaning. I thought India would provide some answers, and it has. The spiritual quest I have been on is a good one, and I have met so many teachers. I learned about love from a special friend I met on a Kibbutz. But there is violence in this world, and I felt it, and that violence can be manifested in aggression or ancestral passing down of destructive traits. I need to better understand where this comes from.

Nodding his head, the minister said, "The world would be so much better if we could find a way of reducing that violence."

I nodded. "Yes, and as we have been talking, I realized that spiritual happiness needs to have a sturdy psychological foundation. And for me, I realize my parents are doing the best they can, and recognize they were affected by their parents and ancestors who passed down ways of dealing with problems that were not always healthy or constructive. I also need to forgive myself for harboring resentment. Forgiveness appears to be a good starting point for this journey."

The minister summarized my insights, "Sounds like your spiritual trip was tied to resolving these issues you had growing up."

"Very true. I know I can have a life of purpose and a life that is fulfilled but I also realize the seeds of love and aggression are within me. They have been passed down to me, and I need to be aware of their existence so I do not harm others or myself."

"I am glad you survived this journey. Sounds like you've made important insights that will help you in life as you find work that will be satisfying."

He pulled over as we had reached our destination, and I got out of his car, "Thank you for listening and giving me the ride. I much appreciate your kindness. Everyone I met, every experience, has been enormously helpful to me as I try to make sense of it all."

At the airport, I boarded the plane and headed back to the states. The person sitting next to me on the flight was named Gloria, a woman with a fun, sarcastic demeanor and dark eyes that sparkled with intelligence and street smarts. We chatted about my trip and my dad the comic. She asked me if I knew any of his jokes, and I told her a few that included me.

"The biggest thrill of all is when you find out you're a proud father for the first time. I'll never forget when they said 'Jay, it's a bouncing boy, 8 pounds, 6 ounces.' I ran to the hospital maternity ward, and there behind the glass are all these screaming babies, and they picked my baby up, and I saw him for the first time. You should have seen him, ugly! I said, 'Put him back, he ain't finished.' That was 8 years ago; you should see him today. Nobody knows the trouble I've seen, and he's finished. And our kids are wonderful, and they want to make changes, and change is progress. My boy comes home and he says, 'Hey man.' And he's looking at my wife. So we finish an argument, and he says, 'I didn't ask to be born.' I looked at him and said: 'It's a lucky thing, I would have turned you down.' My son then said: 'I want to clean up this mess the world is in.' I said, 'Go upstairs to your room, start there.'"

Gloria and I laughed. I mentioned to her, "In bringing humor to the world, everyone surrounding my dad would ultimately be included in his witty monologues. I had mixed feelings about his jokes that involved myself or my family. Perhaps one of the tragic ironies of many comics is that in trying to make people laugh and enjoy themselves, those who are closest to the comedians are inevitably brought into the critical scrutiny of their comics' vision."

Dreaming

As the flight continued, I fell asleep and had a vivid dream that has since stuck with me like a memory.

My mother and father are sitting in our living room and discussing the day's events when my mother turns to my father and says, "I have brain damage now from all the medication they are giving me."

"It's sedated you," my father says, "not brain damage. Maybe we can lower the medication so you can go up to the mountains again? We could go swimming, play ping-pong, and do all the other things we used to do together."

"I'm not a whole person. I'm sitting here and I'm ill."

My father asks, "What do you mean by ill? Do you have pain anywhere?"

She shakes her head. "What this means is that I have to be quieter, not more active. It's too bad I have problems."

My mother points to family heirlooms, "This is a big treasure chest we have here. Your sister Ceal has been taking things from the house."

My father sighs with a heavy head in his hands. "No one is taking things."

"It makes me sick just talking about it." My mother grew visibly upset as she thought about my aunt Ceal coming to the house every month and taking more of her stuff.

"You are making up problems Lynn. The biggest problem we have in this house is medication for you."

"The pills have side effects. My heart pains, I've gained weight, my ankles are swollen. You forced me to stay in a house like this. It's too small. You then tell Ceal that there is too much stuff here, and we need to get rid of it. I had seventeen pillows, now I have seven. Who took them? I just think you're a very dangerous man."

My dad asks, "In what way?"

"You're not my friend. I prove something to you, then you tell me I'm all wet."

My dad replies, "Your dad was an alcoholic and your mother was disturbed, and this problem is in your genes. Medication is the way to help your problems. My biggest problem is your peace of mind."

My mother laughs. "Your biggest problem is your peace of mind."

"Talking can't help. There is nothing that makes sense in what you say."

My mom says, "There were years when I thought you had a girlfriend, you were kidding me. You'd say on the stage, 'My wife and my girlfriend.' And then you'd say that's the girlfriend at that bar, and that's the girlfriend at that bar. I imagined you had a girlfriend, and I didn't know where she was. I was looking for her. This wasn't a mental problem; you set the stage for this thing. And it's awfully hard when you set the stage for me to disprove something I thought you did. And when we went to the mountains, you introduced my girlfriend Shirley as your girlfriend. You'd say, 'This is my wife and this is my girlfriend.' So I wondered if you were playing around with Shirley."

My dad responds, "You know nothing about humor. One of the key areas is the relationship between husbands with their wives. You can only make this type of humor when you are in love with your wife."

My mom says, "I was going through a stressful time. Going up to the mountains, I would ask you 'Is that the one? Is that the one?' And you would kid back, and say 'No, she's that one.' And I was at the point where I was disturbed about it, and you didn't sense it."

My dad looks at my mom and says, "All your life you saw your father cheat on his wife, and now you thought this carried over into our life. You thought I was the same way as your father. Right from the beginning, I did these types of jokes. I joked about girlfriends, but your father actually did it. These jokes are the way I made my living. How is it that affairs didn't happen during the first twenty years of our life? Why are you so sensitive now? It all has to do with chemistry and the mind. As soon as the psychiatrist prescribed certain medications for you, you cleared up, so it has nothing to do with what I was saying."

My mother defiantly says, "You say I might be put away but I have a son who would never let that happen."

And the spotlight on my mom and dad sitting in our living room went out. I was back in the darkness of my sleeping mind.

I woke up as we were about to land. I sat in my seat, beside a stranger named Gloria, and looked out the window at the tarmac. Thinking of the dream, I often felt that my father was so hard on people that at times he ground away at those around him. Perhaps my mother had collapsed under my father's pressure.

We landed at about 6 p.m. on Saturn Airways in New York City, the same terminal I had departed for London. My parents greeted me at the airport where they both burst into tears as they saw me get off the plane. I knew they cared about me and there was a tremendous amount of love and caring between us. My summer had officially ended.

Chapter 6: Finding Wisdom

Epilogue

For the next few years, I was a graduate student in clinical psychology at the University of Rochester. Dave was my classmate and one of my best friends. He was of average height with probing brown eyes and had an intensity with whatever he did. Following graduate school, we would regularly meet at psychology conferences, where he occasionally asked about my trip to India.

Below is one of our conversations at a vegetarian restaurant in New York City. The place was packed with the lunch crowd—well-dressed and well-to-do. And the numerous conversations echoed off the stark, modern furniture and high ceiling.

Dave shook his head, "Will never forget you showing up for graduate school in your hippie clothes, with long hair, a beard, and shorts. The other classmates thought you had accidentally wandered in from outside. We all thought to ourselves, 'who the hell is this guy?' You didn't have the preppy look we had, with jackets and more formal attire."

I smiled in memory of that day. "I'd just come back from my trip to India, and after my travels and work on a Kibbutz, I didn't care about what I was wearing or how I looked on that orientation day."

Dave sipped his latte. "Your trip to India was amazing."

I trickled cream into my Earl Grey tea. "Yes, a remarkable summer."

"I remember you telling me about your Finnish girlfriend at the Kibbutz."

My Friend Dave

"She is wonderful, and I love her for so many reasons, as she helped me get in touch with my feelings and my past. We're still friends, but she's now married in Finland and has a family."

"What were you looking for on this trip?"

"As in James Joyce's and Thomas Mann's writings, I was trying to find my center, my core, where neither fear nor desire could move me."

Dave leaned back in his chair. "You lost me there."

"I was on a quest up my magic mountain to find meaning in my life. I had initially looked for spiritual masters to help me find a purpose."

"Did you need to go all the way to India to do that, and just on your own?"

"Yes, I needed to take this trip without anyone. I felt like when Ibsen's Peer Gynt peeled an onion. There were so many layers to get to the kernel, and maybe there were only layers that kept getting smaller. I had to strip myself of all protections to find what I was looking for."

"And what was that?"

"Over time, I realized I was also on a journey to unravel wounds that stemmed from my family, and in particular my relationship with my dad."

"Your dad, the comic in the Catskills?"

"Yep. He can be gentle and loving, but also easy to anger."

"Can you tell me more?"

"Sure, he has stood by my mother during years when she was weak and sick. He loves his family and would do anything for them. He cares about others, and he genuinely tries to make the world a more enjoyable place through his humor. However, he is demanding and critical."

"Sorry to hear that about that."

"Thanks. His strength and temper can be overwhelming."

"Any idea how he got to be that way?"

"I guess he was the victim of his grandfather's and mother's interpersonal styles that tended to be easy to anger and explosive. His profession also makes him somewhat callous as what was important was to get a laugh, even at anyone's expense."

"So, what can you do in this situation?"

"I guess my job is to learn to see my dad's bravery and generosity, along with his darker side and his anger, and to recognize these domains are also within me."

Dave sighed. "That's heavy."

"Yup, no la-di-da stuff here. I've been reading Robert Bly's book *Iron John* where he eloquently summarizes two tendencies in our fathers. If we adopt psychological thinking toward our father, we can bring out of ourselves forgiveness, complication, humor, symbolic subtlety, and compassion. Out heart begins to melt. We understand how little love the father got. We take his childhood traumas into account. No father will be good all the way."

"Good points and I've been meaning to read that book."

"Mythology helped me see the dark side of my father and his effects on my mom," I said. "I do all I can to help support my mother and will try to live my life in a way that the fate that befell my mother will not happen to me."

"How do you plan on doing that?"

I took a moment to reflect, "I'll avoid being put in a position where someone as strong as my father can undermine me, and thus will avoid the problems experienced by my mom."

"I can see that steady strength you have in everything you do."

I nodded. "Thanks. I also recognize that some of the best and worst qualities of my family are handed down to me, and I am alert to those darker sides."

"You have a different perspective than most," Dave added. "Where does that all come from?"

EXPERIENCING SACREDNESS: A PSYCHO-SPIRITUAL JOURNEY

I looked out the window for a moment. "In my studies since that summer trip, I learned that thousands of years ago, people had more certainty about their life and what would happen after they died. For them, the earth was the center of the universe and humans had been created by God."

"That has certainly changed."

"Yes, when Galileo and Darwin showed we are just one small insignificant planet, and we are descended from chimpanzees. For me, meaning could no longer be obtained from above but needs to be created from within."

Dave cupped his chin. "I wonder what that means to be so connected to this animal world of apes and chimps?"

"It helps us understand where some of our darker sides come from."

Dave chuckled. "If I were a chimp, I'd be privy to being able to reach far enough to scratch that elusive spot in the middle of my back."

"Guess that would be one advantage. But seriously, when Jane Goodall observed chimpanzees in Africa, she provided us with interesting clues about the ancestors of our species."

"Like what?"

"Chimpanzees' abundant energy, playfulness, and vitality are characteristics that reside naturally within us, and these vibrant inner resources can supply the fuel for an animated and spirited life. They also have sex all the time and no one cares to look or comment."

Dave laughed. "Free love, man, makes sense to me."

"But there is also a darker side. Goodall also observed tribes of chimpanzees systematically killing members of other groups and aggressively protecting their territory against others. So, often a dominant chimpanzee would act aggressively to show others he was on top of the social hierarchy."

"You think this has anything to do with humans?"

"Yes. These aggressive animal tendencies reside within our genetic makeup and can lead to vulnerabilities in our efforts to live in a civilized world."

"Did you realize any of this on your trip to India?"

"Yes, as I saw this aggressiveness in a car door that swung open that almost hit me, and my money being stolen and American Express refusing to refund it."

"But with all that violence you saw in your travels, you still were able to find something spiritual."

"That is true, and I now know that transcendence and sacredness are always available, but many never experience these states due to their dark side."

"Can you elaborate?"

"Remember me telling you about the supposed holy man who tried to molest me? It was a shocking reminder of this, as was the sorrow that was expressed by a man named Jean who I met at a Paris bookstore."

"Is that violence also connected with what you have seen in your family?"

"There is a dark side that I had to understand on my trip, including within my family, regarding my dad's anger that was expressed toward my mother."

EXPERIENCING SACREDNESS: A PSYCHO-SPIRITUAL JOURNEY

Dave drummed his fingers on the table. "I see that violent side in so many things that we deal with in our work."

"Sadly, it happens throughout our society as we murder souls when we allow children to go hungry and when we pollute our planet and burn fossil fuels without a sense of connectedness and reverence for nature."

Dave sighed. "Very depressing, and I sometimes think about throwing up my hands and giving up."

I countered, "I don't think the solution is giving up. We can try to make a difference, but I believe we first have to recognize that dark side."

"You mean the evil that is in the world?"

"I don't think there is evil in nature. Think of a fly caught in a spider's web. The web is beautiful, and the spider's dance to the prey is awe-inspiring. We can witness wonderful sights in nature. Now if you're the fly, you wouldn't feel too good about your plight, but that's our burden as well as our joy."

"Yep, I would not want to be a spider's next meal. I hate spiders, and just thinking about that gives me chills. So, how do you integrate all these ideas?"

I sipped the last of my tea. "At its core, my metaphysical journeys helped me realize that the world is a golden sacred lotus, hidden only by the illusions woven by my ego's eyes. Breaking through the ego limitations allowed me to behold paradise."

"You're not taking drugs, are you?"

"Drugs can hint at these alternative ways of seeing the world, but they're not sustainable."

"Tell me more about this paradise," Dave asked.

"These special journeys can end at a place where desire and fear no longer operate, where I had a sense of compassion and empathy for the terror and suffering that are part of this world, and where I was now free to experience the awe and mystery of the universe."

"You experienced this on your trip?"

"I had moments of this insight when I observed a bank guard in London greeting his customers, and even when I escaped the danger of a ferocious dog trying to attack me."

Dave shook his head. "Still not sure I understand this. It's mighty complicated."

"Let me try again. My journey was an effort to integrate the many different sides of myself. But the final stage, the metaphysical journey, is the most challenging. It involves coming to terms with the world of sorrow, the world of human beings attempting to act in civilized ways but often resorting to aggression as wild as any animal in the jungle."

"When I look at the world and think we're far worse than any animal."

"What do you mean?"

Dave shrugged. "Animals don't kill gleefully and on a mass scale by dropping 5-ton bombs on helpless people. They obey a basic instinct that we've abused in ways no chimpanzee ever will."

"Joseph Campbell's work with mythology has helped me come to terms with this."

Dave took the last bite of his bagel and cream cheese. "Wasn't he the guy who influenced Lucas' Star Wars?"

"Yeah, he was a professor of literature at Sarah Lawrence College. He just left his doctoral studies when his advisors would not support his studies in medieval literature, Sanskrit, and modern art."

"That takes guts to leave a doctoral program."

"For Campbell, the solution to our dilemma is to be grounded in eternity. By realizing the eternal is within us, we can disengage and later re-engage as participants with joy in the sorrows of the world."

Dave was a good listener and had a genuine concern for me and humanity. Our conversations allowed me to express some of what I had learned during my journey to India.

The Mythological Journey

Over the years after my summer trip, I continued searching for answers to questions of

existence in mythology, psychoanalysis, existentialism, philosophy, ecology, religion, and in particular Buddhism (See Appendix D for more of my thoughts on mythology and Appendix E for the origins of violence). I now knew there was meaning in a mythological interpretation of the world, which began with my trip to India.

I had another conversation with Dave over lunch at an Italian restaurant, in a dimly lit room with velvet curtains cushioning the walls, a chandelier centering the eatery, and a shiny black piano in the corner. It was early evening, and we pretty much had the place to ourselves.

Dave asked, "Can you tell me more about Campbell?"

"Sure, Joseph Campbell's writings helped me understand dilemmas in our nature. We must face the reality that we consume and will be consumed. That is nature's gift and blessing. It can set us free or make us curse our days."

Dave frowned. "Dying's a bummer. I'm not sure how that can be a gift from nature."

The waiter arrived with a warm baguette and a dish with soft butter. I slathered a slice and said, "Maybe this will help. Campbell told the story of an Indian myth that showed our mixed burdens of being both animals and spiritual beings. A tiger dies giving birth to a baby tiger. Some goats see the helpless baby tiger and decide to adopt it. A year later, an older tiger sees the goats and the young tiger playing. Alarmed at this sight, the older tiger struts over, grabs the young tiger and brings him over to a pond so the young tiger can see his reflection in the water. The older tiger says: 'You look like me. You're a tiger, not a goat.'

The older tiger brings the younger one back to his cave and stuffs fresh meat down the young tiger's throat. The young tiger gives his first tiger roar."

Dave nibbled on a slice of bread. "Interesting, but what does it mean?"

"Campbell used this story to show our two natures, one the tiger and the other a goat. The goat symbolizes civilization, which is a thin veneer, but the tiger nature is below each of us. We all have to deal with our tiger aggressiveness while living in a society of goats."

"I see. Can you share another story about this?"

The waiter arrived with two steaming bowls of minestrone that smelled of ripe tomatoes and basil.

EXPERIENCING SACREDNESS: A PSYCHO-SPIRITUAL JOURNEY

"Okay, a scorpion asked a frog to give him a ride across a river. The frog replied he would, but the scorpion would have to promise not to sting him. The scorpion agreed but when they got to the middle of the river, the scorpion stung the frog.

"Why did you bite me?" the frog asks. "Now we're both gonna drown and die."

The scorpion says, "I was only acting in my nature."

Dave frowned. "That is rather dark, as both died."

"The scorpion had a dark side just as we do, and our journey involves recognizing it so it does not destroy us."

Dave slurped his soup. "I'm not sure what all this means?"

"I'm also still trying to figure it out. Joseph Campbell believed myths are the way the unconscious communicates with the conscious self, to deal with some of the basic issues of life. The dream I told you I had when I was flying home from India about a tense conversation between my parents was rich in symbolic imagery of the issues I have had to face."

"This stuff is worth contemplating. What book has Campbell written?"

"His best-known work is *The Hero with a Thousand Faces*."

"What's it about?"

"The inner journey begins with a recognition that something is wrong with the nature of the inner self. This felt incongruity or tension is a call to adventure, in which each person must travel a route no one has journeyed before, and why I needed to take my journey alone."

"What was the purpose of your trip?"

"To find what is missing, that deepest sense of harmony, the mystery that captures my imagination and holds it so time passes without me noticing it."

"I guess we all are searching for something like this," Dave said, "Can you give me another example from Campbell?"

"A famous myth is the Sir Galahad story, about knights in King Arthur's Court. These knights saw a group of angels carrying the Holy Grail covered by a cloth and decided to embark on a quest to find the Grail. They considered it a disgrace to set forth as a group, so each entered the forest where it was darkest, where there was no visible path, and where there was no one to lead the way. In other words, the quest was an individual journey."

"Your journey to India was like a mythical trip."

"Yes, and the dragons I encountered were parts of myself I needed to incorporate. If this mythical trip was to succeed, I needed to begin to divest my social roles to follow my path."

"I wonder if all the great myths have this underlying message?"

"Even Homer's Odysseus, the first great epic of Western literature, deals with this."

Dave asked me to share the tale.

"The story begins after Odysseus' victory at Troy. As he was returning home, he and his men stopped at a town where they raped the women and plundered and robbed the citizens. The gods disapproved of this behavior and summoned winds to blow him to the beginning of his soul journey. On his trip to the underworld, Odysseus first had to divest himself of his prior beliefs and lifestyle. On his travels within the underworld or the unconscious, Odysseus gradually learned women could not be treated as pieces of property."

"How did he learn this?"

"On the isle of Calypso, Odysseus lived with a nymph in a mature relationship. To survive and complete the journey, he was compelled to incorporate aspects of himself he had previously rejected. With his new insights, he was ready to return to the real world and Penelope, his wife. Through his journey, Odysseus developed a more mature and healthy relationship with women."

"I see. By integrating the opposite poles of our nature and accepting the paradoxes inherent in human existence, we could begin to embrace and love all aspects of ourselves."

I nodded. "I think so. In many myths, the hero meets a dark force, usually a black knight, a dragon, or a whale, who represents the rejected aspect of the self. That dark force was my dad, and my task was the hero's task, which was to integrate the opposite aspects of myself. Myths can move people, as they did me, by speaking to their souls."

Dave wiped his empty soup bowl with a slice of bread. "Where do spiritual ideas and the reason for your trip fit in?"

"As you know, I was looking for something spiritual on my journey but realized that even in my faith, there was a mystical tradition where God's divine sparks were everywhere, and spiritual love, unity, peace, and joy could occur during prayer."

"It is also in other religions, right?"

The waiter finally arrived with my spaghetti with veggies in marinara sauce and Dave's ravioli. By the look and smell, the wait was worthwhile.

"Yes, in Christianity's gospel according to Saint Thomas, the Kingdom of God is described as being right in front of us, a vision we usually don't see because of the enchantment of the eyes. The Christ figure disenchants us by opening our eyes. The Buddha also releases people from the enchantment of Maya, or illusion."

"Do all mythologies have these types of underlying messages?"

"I doubt scholars in the field of mythology would agree with there being comparable underlying messages, but there are helpful teachings from the mystical side of many religious traditions."

"Can you give me any more details about this?"

"Sure, as an example, Anderson and Hopkins believe there are multiple paths to seeing the divine in ordinary life. What appears to be common to those seeking a sacred life is a connection to being present in day-to-day activities, as I experienced when the elderly man cried when he thought I was his son."

"That makes sense."

"It does. A cyclical process often occurs, with people, at times, feeling confident and other times feeling confused. But there is always an ability to see the larger whole even in despair or crisis, which I frequently experienced during my trip. There were always opportunities to see the divine in everyday life."

"Any other scholars who have done work in this area?"

"Yes, Schwartz also describes the process of being on the spiritual path as more important than any outcome, and it's a path that involves going forward, slipping, and trying again. Both psychological and spiritual practices can be used together on this journey to the realization of wisdom."

Dave shrugged. "I get nervous about some of these spiritual journeys. There are so many abuses that happened with cults, including polygamy, incest, and violence toward women."

I nodded. "Many cults do engage in these terrible transgressions, and whenever one group has power over others, whether it is religious leaders or the police, our dark side can have unfortunate consequences."

Dave summed up our conversation by saying, "We gotta keep our feet on the ground and have our issues under control, to be sure that we don't perpetuate more tragedy."

"Wonderful analysis and I do feel that is what I came home with, a new appreciation for these issues."

Trying to Understand My Family

Living with a bigger-than-life father can provide many challenges, as the more power a person has, the more the dark side can seep out in unexpected ways. Comedians are on stage 24 hours a day, with a need for attention and approval, but when minor irritations mount for not receiving adoration, a simmering volcano can explode.

To most people, my dad was seen as witty, bright, and well-connected. People with power can often be seen differently by the external world compared to how they're seen by their families. So it was with my dad, who was pleased when he was the centerpiece. This was reinforced by the public which provided him with unconditional support and approval.

Because of his exciting life, my dad attracted more attention than most of us, but mythology helps us understand a darker side. During one visit to my folks, I had a chance to see my dad perform at the Concord, a well-known Catskill hotel.

His humor often reflected his experiences in our family, as reflected in this joke:

"I don't know about you, but for me the worst word in the English language is divorce. Divorce. When you promise to love, honor, and obey till death do us part. You don't want to see a divorce. You want to see her die." As the audience laughed, my dad would distance himself from this statement by saying, "I don't think so. It's just a joke. Just a joke."

The audience that night gave my dad a standing ovation. The Catskills audience loved his humor.

After the show, as we began driving home, I asked my dad about several of his jokes involving my mom including: "I have a wife and a wonderful girlfriend, oh she's not really that wonderful."

My dad chuckled. "Comedians get their best material from their families, and you know I have done this for my entire career."

"But dad, you have a wife with serious paranoia, and she thinks you are telling the truth about having a girlfriend."

"She doesn't know what she's saying, and it's a chemical imbalance in her head. That's what the psychiatrist says."

"You've got hundreds of jokes and the audience loves them. Don't you think you could hold off on these, particularly when mom goes with you to a show?"

"It has nothing to do with me or my jokes. She has a mental disorder, and that's her problem. I love her and will do anything for her, but my routines have nothing to do with her condition."

"You could be right," I responded, "and your jokes have nothing to do with her condition. But just maybe these jokes along with your lack of encouragement for her to become the independent businesswoman might have contributed to her problems."

Becoming irate, my dad snapped. "Nonsense, and she has no business sense at all. I've given her money to throw away at plenty of things over the years, so just don't bring that up."

My dad continued, "You see people can have these fears when they have been attacked or molested but in fact, they have not had any harm done to them. Nothing has happened to her to give her these fears except the sickness, the chemicals in her brain being off. Point out something I have done that has been dangerous. Point out one thing. I have never tried to cheat her out of anything. She's had everything she's ever wanted monetarily."

I replied, "If a person feels they are considered inadequate and irrational by someone close to them eventually they—"

"Become that."

We sit with this for a moment. My dad and I held the weight of this quiet moment in our minds.

"When she says something to you like 'I have these types of concerns' and you say to her 'The concerns are all because of chemical imbalances in the head,' can you see how she would say that is not a supportive statement?"

"Well, would you want me to lie to her and go along with her and say, 'yes you are right?'"

I replied, "But she feels this way and you feel she is irrational."

"You can't convince her otherwise?"

"You could say you appreciate the fact she has these concerns. That type of statement does provide the person with more respect and support. In other words, by saying you feel that way and the feelings are important—"

"What do you mean I feel that way? I should say 'Maybe you're right?' Couldn't you just tell her she is wrong? This is a certain state of mind. She would put me in jail if she could. She doesn't know what she is doing."

I interjected, "Given the condition she was in at that time, for you to joke about having girlfriends was wrong."

My dad responded, "You are saying that my using this type of humor led to mom having shock treatments, hearing voices, and thinking that someone was out to get her?"

I added, "Dad, your life is about kidding people about issues, some important some not important; that is your personality. Anything about a person's life, you find the humor or the joke in it, you slant it, you tilt it, all at the expense of the other person. It's not all negative; often it is funny, and we can all laugh at the joke. But sometimes the humor is painful."

"You're imagining that; I never said that. When she was hiring detectives and going to the police, calling the ambulance and the fire station, and I was not kidding her at that time."

"Being supportive of her feelings is the key."

My dad grew irritated and says, "Going along with what she is feeling is absolute nonsense."

That ended our conversation about his jokes and my mom. I tried many times to get them into couples therapy, but those sessions never brought up any substantial changes in their relationship.

My parents were drawn together and loved each other deeply, but neither was able to satisfy the other's psychological needs. My dad loved the fact that my mom adored him, but he wanted her to stay at home and raise children, and not have an independent life as a businesswoman. My dad's temper, passed on from his mom and grandfather, along with his need to be the center of attention, made it difficult for my mother to have a separate and independent identity.

My Mother Passes Away

During my mom's last years, she was hospitalized repeatedly for different ailments. Each time, she had rallied, beating the odds, and challenging the doctors who had given up on her so long ago. At long last, she died. At her funeral, as I looked at my mom in her casket, she had a remarkable sense of peace and tranquility. My dad was sobbing. Tears rolled down my cheeks.

I was asked to eulogize at the funeral. The immediate family walked into the chapel and sat in the front row. The rabbi began his sermon. His voice was clear and resolute and defied the wrinkles on his worn face. My dad's trembling hands were on my back. The rabbi mentioned that my mom had been a pioneer in the "garage sale" movement and had been one of the key promoters giving rise to their popularity. I knew my mom would have chuckled at my insertion of this anecdote into the rabbi's talk.

Picture of my Mother

The rabbi asked me to say a few words. My heart was pounding as I rose and saw the chapel was filled. For years, my dad had been boasting about his son to all his friends and relatives. I was sure there was nothing I could now say that might match what he had portrayed me to be. I stood before the podium, my mom's casket to my left, and my dad softly crying in front of me.

I put my head down, had no script to read, and felt alone and unprepared. My throat was choked with emotions as I raised my head and looked at the audience. I knew that my entire life had been a preparation for this moment. This would be my last tribute to my mom. I was now a reflection of her. I symbolized her life. I was the appointed guide, a messenger to transmit a glimpse of a remarkable woman, one who some had only known as a chronically sick person.

I had one phrase that stuck in my mind and that I knew would start my recollections of my mom's life:

"I sometimes wonder what greatness means. Often it's seen in the little things."

All my fears and anxieties had now vanished. I needed no script. The words came to me with power and vigor I had never previously experienced. The words were given to me as a gift and I knew that whatever I stated would be right. I was now looking at the audience that filled the funeral home. It seemed like hours had passed, but it had only been seconds. I was in a trance. Time stood still.

"When I was in elementary school, my family moved to Teaneck, New Jersey. Entering the fifth grade, I quickly began experiencing academic problems, as this school system was more academically advanced than my prior school. Stumbling academically, I also began getting into trouble with my peers both in and out of class. Rather than allow those early academic and social problems to accumulate, my mom acted decisively. She got me a tutor and a therapist. Within a few months, I was caught up academically and my relationships with peers improved."

"My mother was years ahead of her time in recognizing the importance of prevention. Instinctively she was able to identify problems at an early point and correct them before they became more enduring and difficult to overcome. Later when I entered graduate school to become a clinical psychologist, I was drawn to the preventive side of psychology. Why were so many of our clinical efforts directed toward the repair of dysfunction and remediation?"

"My first National Institute of Mental Health grant, for over a million dollars, had its genesis in my mom's idea. She had helped me so gracefully during my school transition. Perhaps I could take this lesson and extend it to others. My federally funded project involved providing elementary school transfer students with a comprehensive preventive intervention. Children who entered a new school were provided an orientation program, a buddy, and tutoring to catch up academically. These types of programs have now been established in many school systems. The generative ideas for the work came from a mother who wanted to help me adjust to a difficult transition."

I looked at the casket, "Thank you, Mom."

"When I was about seven years old, my mom and I went to a carnival. I already had all types of pets, from snakes to cats and dogs when I said to my mom, "Why don't we get a chimp?"

Mom replied, "Fine."

"I brought the chimp to school for show and tell, and years later, people still remind me about bringing this pet to school."

"The reason I mention this episode is that my mom was always open to the possibilities. Her attitude was 'why not?' Within her unconventional way, I saw at this early age, a world that had few barriers or limitations. Our imaginations and willingness to take risks were a natural and fundamental way of life. Whether it was collecting coins, stamps, or rocks, or purchasing contemporary art, she affirmed life and opened my eyes to a world of discovery and adventure."

EXPERIENCING SACREDNESS: A PSYCHO-SPIRITUAL JOURNEY

Again, I turned to the casket, "Thank you, Mom."

"When I was even younger, I was quite an overactive child. Living in Washington DC, my mom had her hands full trying to figure out what I was up to, as my cousin Sid Roth can attest. At age four I was given my first costume, a Superman outfit. I had dreamt about flying with the birds and was convinced this costume would allow me to actualize my dreams. Bouncing on my bed, it became clear to me that I was able to fly, even if only for the briefest period. With my sister looking on in amusement, I opened a window, tied a pillow to my stomach, and grabbed an umbrella. I reckoned that if the power I had been given with the Superman costume for some reason failed me, the umbrella would allow me to gently float to Earth and land on a pillow. When I got on the window ledge, several stories above the ground, my sister dashed downstairs to inform my mother of my dangerous plans. With the umbrella inflated and the pillow securely fastened to my stomach, I was seconds away from an untimely death. My mother miraculously appeared and somehow coached me down from the windowsill. I was not punished for this life-threatening feat, but my mother would now keep an even closer eye on my movements and plans. She saved my life on this occasion."

"This was not the only time my mother protected me. Using a sixth sense that only a mother can know, she gave of herself unselfishly and repeatedly, often at her peril, to be there for me."

Once again, I looked at the casket and said, "Thank you, Mom."

"Few people endured the pain and suffering that my mom faced daily. As you know, she had multiple illnesses, any one of which would have killed others with less fortitude. Some of you only knew her during her time of declining health. It was so easy to overlook her vital soul and spirit during these years. Isn't it remarkable that even in excruciating discomfort, my mom never spoke a foul or profane word? She was a profile in courage. She never looked to the heavens and asked, 'Why hath thou forsaken me?' Instead, she focused her attention on experiencing what was beautiful about life, the wonders always in front of her, just as they are for us. She never asked for sympathy or pity. She never complained. If someone tried to get her to talk about her ailments, she might respond, 'What's the big deal?' You see, for my mom, life was a wondrous journey, an adventure to be lived even if in unrelenting pain. There were articles to read, investments to make, and life to experience. Her will to live, her affirmation of life, and her courage in pain are her mythic gifts to us."

"When any of us experience common afflictions and tragedies, we can look to my mom as a role model. Through her grace, we have the potential to peacefully deal with the most difficult times. This mild-mannered, soft-spoken, unpretentious humble woman is a veritable hero. With a crumbling body, her spirits continued to soar—showing us we can be truly healthy regardless of the conditions of our bodies."

"Through years of marriage, she enjoyed an unparalleled and intense relationship with her husband. This was no infatuation; this was the deepest bond of love, and most of us would be fortunate to have one-tenth of what they experienced. And there were sparks, which always accompany intensity, but the unconditional commitment was a wonder. This was a union that few can ever fully understand, but none can refute the love and affection that was so strikingly visible."

My parents were very much in love

"And when my dad had a show to perform in the Catskills, my mom, who could barely walk, would somehow manage to sneak into my dad's car, so that she could be beside him for the trip to the mountains. With her last burst of energy, she wanted to be by his side - giving to the end."

I paused and looked down for several seconds, "Sometimes I wonder what greatness means. Perhaps it's seen in the little things."

My tribute complete, I sat down. My attempt to eulogize my mother, however well-meaning, would never come close to the honor and praise she deserved. Words can never truly encapsulate our love for another person. Many approached me later and thanked me for my heartfelt tribute. I accepted the praise but knew the words had been a gift, the final one from my mom.

For the first month after my mom's death, my dad was clinically depressed. He stopped doing shows and stayed in his house day and night. There was an oil painting of my mom on the dining room table. My dad stared at it, often placing his hand on the painting and then kissing his fingers as if he had touched his tallis to the Torah during a religious event.

"Lenny, life is just not worth it now that Lynn is gone."

"Dad, she was a remarkable person and we both were so blessed to have her in our lives."

"I can't entertain anymore. I just feel too sad and will never get back on the stage."

"Dad, you love being an entertainer and there are thousands of people who still want to hear your jokes."

"I just can't make people laugh anymore. Lynn was always there, always listening to me, always my best critic and friend."

"Yes, she was a beautiful person in so many ways."

A few months later, my dad began accepting club dates again. At the end of his first show, he dedicated the show to his late wife and cried on stage. He slowly began reentering life. At the end of his performance, he would return to his dressing room and cry. He was now so alone. The woman he had battled for so many years was now consuming him, obsessing him, troubling him. As if from her grave, she was instilling some of the pain she had for so long endured from him. His anger and fury no longer had her as a target, and now it was reflected, a trauma as severe as anything he had ever inflicted on her.

EXPERIENCING SACREDNESS: A PSYCHO-SPIRITUAL JOURNEY

A year before he died, he entertained at a New Jersey seaside resort by the Atlantic Ocean. His memory was failing and he began repeating jokes. That was his last official performance.

A relative called me one morning, and I instinctively knew it was about my dad. The words came out of the phone. "Lenny, your dad died last night. Peacefully."

I was overwhelmed. I could not say anything. A part of me had also died. I put the phone down and cried with a sense of emptiness as if my life force had suddenly evaporated into thin air.

Since his death, I have often reflected on his presence and all his wonderful and flawed qualities. My journey was to forgive myself for not being able to do more for my parents, and for my lack of tolerance for their limitations. Their residues will forever remain within me, and my task is to retain the best, such as their love and caring, but try to recognize and limit the darker sides of anger and violence.

In part to remember my dad, I edited 60 of his routines on YouTube (https://www.youtube.com/user/JayJasonTribute), and over 50,000 people have continued to enjoy his humor over time. He's probably looking down from heaven asking me why I shared his material for free.

My parents tried as best as they could to provide my sister and me with the foundations of our lives. They also taught me that marriage and its ups and downs aren't for the faint of heart. Marriage, like a rare orchid, requires constant care and attention. My parents undoubtedly loved each other but sometimes even love is not enough for a healthy relationship. Husband and wife need to be compatible and exercise empathy as much as possible. It's a fine and complicated balance.

Final thoughts on Healing and Forgiveness

The journey I undertook from England to India would be impossible to embark on today, as this trip occurred before the wars with Iran and Afghanistan, before 9/11, and before the Islamic radicalization that escalated in the late 1970s. With two superpowers engaged in a political dance that dominated the world scene in the early 1970s, Europe and the Middle East were relegated to the sidelines. Consequently, many of the customs and traditions I witnessed had been undisturbed for centuries. At that time, Iran was still ruled by the Shah, and Afghanistan even had a king. There was a thirst for information about "America" among many of the people I encountered and a justifiable cynicism and fear of what my presence and the "U.S." represented. However, I was less threatening as a foreigner with few possessions except my backpack and thus was greeted with less suspicion and more openness, which allowed me an unparalleled glimpse into their daily lives.

During my long rides through vast deserts and enigmatic lands, I had time to reflect on the fine line between inspiration and tragedy. I will never forget the elderly man in the former Yugoslavia, sitting by a roadside outdoor café, waving his hands furiously toward me, trying to invite me to join him for lunch. He cried as we ate, as I looked like his son who had long since died. I also learned about sacredness from the experiences of mystics, monks, and religious leaders, and about mysticism traditions within Islam, Christianity, Hinduism, Buddhism, and Judaism involving some form of contact with the transcendent.

I also witnessed unimaginable poverty, as when a mother pushed her baby toward me, saying: "Give me some money or my baby will die." During the trip, my money was stolen, I got get sick drinking the local water, I was severely bitten by insects, and even a holy man in India tried to molest me. I sometimes wondered whether I was capable of enduring these types of hardships. At times, I was unsure why I needed to take on such an arduous, mysterious personal journey. But I knew I needed to strip away all that had previously protected me, which would only be possible if I disconnected from everyone and everything from my past. Only then could I see more clearly what I was searching for on this journey.

I knew I did not want to be like so many people in the U.S. who disliked their jobs and social roles yet maintained a mask because they feared a future without the certainty of their current roles. I saw many dealing with stressful, unsatisfying lifestyles that profoundly depleted their vital energies. I did not want that to happen to me. I needed courage and faith as I began my journey toward authenticity, and I sensed it would help me learn to follow my inner voice, but I needed to learn what my truth might be.

This overland journey involved me confronting imbalances and the debilitating consequences of excess. It also involved learning to balance power and erotic drives or finding a way to make peace with childhood traumas. As with all great myths, this trip connected me with those dimensions of my personality that had been underdeveloped or neglected. My quest had been aroused by an effort to untangle complicated family dynamics, which set the foundations for unfolding my moral and spiritual life. I needed to understand why fundamentally good people often caused such unintentional harm to others.

I had thought maybe I needed to go to graduate school and become a psychologist to find answers to these types of questions, or perhaps I could find the needed guides on my trip to India. At Brandeis University, Abraham Maslow spoke of new images that had more vitality, more energy, and were more intrinsically appealing. His notions of self-actualization acknowledged an appreciation for the mystery of life, and my readings of eastern religions suggested a different reality that involved humans developing even god-like qualities (Appendix F provides more about these wisdom traditions).

At that time and even more so today, people are searching for their true purpose in life, and what might provide them with a meaningful and fulfilled life. I was also passionate and driven by these types of questions that drove me to undertake this rite of passage. It was clear to me during my travels that we live in a materialistic world filled with sorrow, including a disintegration of community and spiritual values, which occurred before the COVID-19 epidemic and the racial tensions. What I witnessed in my journey also applies to our society as millions with chronic illnesses or disabilities lack social support and live in isolation. We have failed those hundreds of thousands of people who are homeless or released from state hospitals and prisons with no place to go. In addition, there are increasing tensions in our society as the gap widens between those who have access to resources versus those who don't, those who are wealthy versus those in poverty, and those with advanced education and technological skills versus those without them. I felt overwhelmed by the problems I saw on my journey, including those that I faced in the U.S. I then realized it will take personal and spiritual transformations to build the inner resources and resilience to find solutions to these pressing problems. Some of the eastern religions can provide a possible solution to reduce the sorrows of the world.

I have learned that psychological healing allows forgiveness and provides a sturdier foundation for experiences of sacredness and a sense of gratitude. By being transported to uncharted terrain, a time in the past, in parts of our world rarely explored, I began my journey of being present in the moment, honoring and experiencing feelings, finding a deeper meaning in life, and beginning to resolve past psychological traumas. This memoir provided me with a fresh and enchanting canvas to better understand, explore, and savor happiness, purpose, and transcendence. There are many paths to sacredness. My summer journey helped me "wake up" to appreciate them.

Gratitude

This is my first effort to reach a broader audience with a fresh and enchanting canvas for understanding and exploring happiness, purpose, meaning, and transcendence. Insights from my trip have been a foundation for my later work, as I have embraced a social action position that features working in collaboration with neighborhoods and organizations to strengthen a community's resourcefulness and problem-solving abilities. Throughout my career, I have been blessed with my many community partners, who have taught me how to appreciate a sense of sacredness.

I owe a debt of gratitude to John Moritsugu and Nicole Porter for writing the Foreword and Afterword. I thank ilan Herman for his encouragement and editorial help as I wrote this book. Donna Thomas and Kitt Hamlen also provided wonderful editorial services. I am also grateful for Harriet Melrose, Julie Rosenbaum, Daryl Isenberg, and Karina Reyes's unflagging and good-natured support, and to Jonathan Shallit, Amanda Valenti, Erica Verrillo, Mrs. Glenn, and Debs Renz for their cogent comments on portions of this book. Carol Booton helped me switch my writing style from an academic tone to "marketing speak."

I would also like to extend thanks to the following individuals who read parts of this volume and offered valuable, constructive feedback: Ken Lipman, Rob Kurson, Sage Huston, Scott Fivelson, Sunamita Lin, Jane Elle, Laurel Ornitz, Danielle Steele, David Jones, David Jerk, Anne Koose, E. Gabriel, Eric Butterman, Robert Damien, Victor H., Alfred Wolfe, and Amy Outland.

No words can fully express the gratitude I feel toward my friends Dave Glenwick, Roger Weissberg, Dn. Joe Ferrari, Stephen Fawcett, Anne

LENNY JASON

Bogat, Kathleen Gibson, Paul Molloy, Brad Olson, Vernita Perkins, Jane Harmon Jacobs, LaVome Robinson, Renee Taylor, Susan McMahon, Olya Glantsman, Susan Torres-Harding, Jean Rhodes, Jean Hill, Tonya Hall, Jean Rhodes, Pamela Woll, Ray Lorion, Howard Kantor, Roberto Requina, Richard Katz, Doreen Salina, John Majer, Chelsea Torres, Ted Bobak, Mayra Guerrero, Jerry Cleland, Arny Reichler, Mary Dimmock, and Chris Keys whose ideas and caring over the years have been such important sources of support and inspiration.

Appendix A: Tumultuous Brandeis Years

When I was an undergraduate at Brandies University, I tutored disadvantaged children, taught blind and deaf infants, and co-taught several psychology courses at Newton High School. In one state hospital, I even spoke with a patient who had been analyzed by the founder of psychoanalysis, Sigmund Freud.

I had gone to Brandeis to study with Abraham Maslow, one of the founders of the Humanistic Psychology movement. His work featured five categories of human needs including physiological needs, safety needs, love, and belonging needs, esteem needs, and self-actualization needs. But the lower survival needs had to be satisfied to go on to higher ones like self-actualization.

Self-actualization was the highest stage in Maslow's theory of human motivation, and it helped drive us to realize our true talents and potentialities. I had an opportunity to be trained in some humanistic approaches by Maslow's colleagues. I also met the gestalt therapist Fritz Perls at a workshop, and participated in a role-playing exercise with him. His work focused on helping people deal with current life challenges rather than past experiences. He also stressed the importance of understanding the context of a person's life.

I took one class with Dr. Krech, who stated in the first class: "My mentor had been taught by Dr. Wundt, the founder of psychology. You are now four generations from the founder of psychology, and by being in this class, I will pass on the mantle to you." Dr. Krech was one of the scientists in the late 1960s that showed that the brains of rats that were provided an enriched environment became six percent thicker than the brains of impoverished rats. My advisor, Dr. Maher, was one of the first behavioral psychopathologists. I also took a course with Dr. Mulholland, one of the first biofeedback practitioners.

My Brandeis years were filled with fun times as well as political activism as illustrated by the continuation of the conversation with Roger and Allen from Chapter 1.

Allen elbowed his way into the conversation. "Remember when we crashed a mixer at Wellesley? Everyone from all those Ivy League schools was there, dressed to the hilt, and we barged into the dance, looking like hippies. Those snobs wouldn't lower themselves to talk to us.

That night remained fresh in my mind for many years. It was the classic example of the caste system in the U.S., a country that claims that no such system exists and that "anyone can succeed if they pull themselves up by their bootstraps and work hard to realize the American Dream." And while that's true to a certain extent, perhaps a minimal one at that, the night we crashed the mixer proved otherwise.

My friends and I wore our scraggly jeans, taking particular pride in the holes that dotted the pants. Our hair was long, our beards scruffy, and we walked in with the swagger reserved for revolutionaries on the march. The greeting from the well-to-do was frosty—rolling eyes, snobbish smirks, noses wrinkled with disgust while the boys strutted by in their polyester pants and polo shirts, the hair in a buzz cut, their cheeks smooth and reeking with expensive cologne. The girls' greetings were worse. They pretended we were never born. I'll admit that some of these girls were ravishing—shiny blonde hair over slender shoulders, prim and proper skirts and dresses, high-heeled shoes that showed long and sculptured legs—they were the cream of the crop of daddy's daughters, and they knew it. And while the revolutionary zeal drove my idealism, I was also young, impressionable, and much prone to the dismissive treatment we received. It's the time in life when one judgmental glance from a pretty girl can tear at your heart.

Allen said, "Then you screamed out your challenge to the hundreds on the lawn, 'Is anybody friendly here?'"

"Mary started waving her arms at us and screamed, 'I am!'" Allen said. "She came over to talk to us, and we had a great time when she gave us a tour of the campus. She was uncomfortable with all the snooty normies at Wellesley and felt these Ivy League settings were impersonal and outta touch. Mary was one special person."

"It was nice meeting someone unpretentious," I said. "What a hoot. I guess we weren't being bred to be leaders of our country like they supposedly were. Who needs that crap anyway? The country's a mess."

Allen reminisced. "That reminds me of a different mixer at Boston University, the night we met Nancy and her friends and took over the Saturday night dance."

I recalled how Boston College was less stuffy than Wellesley. I didn't have to yell for attention, and the women didn't scurry off in disdain. Perhaps the students attending were hoping for our scraggly souls to guide them to loosening up and 'getting down.' Papa Was a Rolling Stone was pumping from the PA and questioned anyone's need to ignore the groove waiting to be interpreted in the clumsy yet well-meaning dance moves typical of white people. I was and remain a shoddy dancer, but my enthusiasm that night compensated for my performance, so much so that people giggled and joined in.

"We convinced everyone to form a big circle and danced wildly to the music. What an outrageous time it was, bringing life and vitality to that dull dance. After that, we had friends to visit whenever we went to Boston. I did some neat stuff there over the years. What an evening!

And that Nancy? She was a sight. Long red hair, you dated her for a few years."

I looked at Allen. "I remember Nancy and that evening."

Nancy was a sweet soul, and I liked her, maybe even loved her, but when I wanted to talk about what I was reading or thinking about, we didn't click that well. I was absorbing so many new ideas and needed a girlfriend with whom I could dialogue and process concepts. We stayed friends but just weren't meant to be together as a couple.

"We've had some amazing times, and as bad as things have been with Vietnam, we at least tried to change things," Roger added.

"Like when you and Rinky created a stir on campus," I said. " I loved that your dog attended classes as he wandered around campus. Everyone knew and loved Rinky. When the Brandeis administration told you Rinky could no longer be on campus, it hit the front pages of our newspaper. It was a wonderful outcome when you took his case to the student judiciary committee, and they ruled in your favor."

"Rinky was one-of-a-kind. I got him from an animal hospital."

I visualized Rinky at play on campus, and Roger continued. "His owner abused him. When I first saw him, the pup looked terrible. They were ready to put him down, and I heard him yelp and cry as I was walking away. I couldn't help but turn back and adopt him. He was always calm and content. I learned lots from him. A real spiritual being."

Allen nodded. "I loved what you did with Rinky and taking on the administration. There has been so much great social activism in the last few years. I was there in 1969 when about 70 black students took over Ford Hall for about ten days. They had ten demands for better minority representation on campus."

"Yeah, the students got amnesty, and the university made some changes in admission procedures and increased scholarships to African-American students," I said.

"Do you remember the dedication of the Usdan Student Center?" Roger asked.

"We embarrassed the President and his cronies by demanding they start a free daycare center available to anyone at Brandeis."

"And last year," I added, "The Puerto Rican and Mexican-American students organized a protest at the Kutz dining hall to support the United Farm Workers' strike against non-unionized lettuce growers."

Allen chimed in, "Those were good times. Job recruiters from Mobil Oil had their session interrupted by SDS. We've been in the midst of a terrific movement."

Roger chuckled, "Wasn't it great when over 300 students signed a petition nominating our own Angela Davis, who I think graduated from Brandeis in 1965, for Alumni Association President?"

Allen got angry. " I can never forgive Nixon for invading Cambodia and widening the Vietnam war. He claimed it was done to disrupt North Vietnamese supply lines, but that's pure bullshit."

"Then the National Guard killed four protesters at Kent State University just a few days later on April 30."

He became vehement as he continued. "More than a million people on over 800 campuses demanded they wouldn't take it anymore. It must have been the largest protest in American history."

I added: "Yeah, students at hundreds of campuses boycotted classes. The Brandeis Asian-American Students Association led the campus dissent. Professor Fellman's office was the headquarters of the National

Student Strike. I was so moved that I hitched down to the protest in Washington, D.C. I was there when the cops confronted the demonstrators with tear gas to disperse the crowds."

I shook my head in fury at the memory. "There was such tension in the crowd. I ran from building to building, trying to stay one step ahead of the police."

I rubbed my head as I remembered the cracked heads of the students. "I'll never forget hitching back to Brandeis. A car stopped on the turnpike, and a passenger leaned out the window, 'We don't have room, but here's a joint.' I put it in my pocket, figured I'd give it to the next person who offered me a ride."

I shrugged as I chuckled at the memory.

"Could you believe it? The next car that pulled over was a cop. I thought I was busted for sure, but fortunately, he just told me to stop hitching and drove on."

Roger chimed in. "That makes me think of my friend, Susan Saxe. I still can't believe what she did."

"Yeah, me neither," I said.

Susan had been active on National Strike Day at Brandeis. I remember having supper with her and some friends when she asked if I wanted to rob a bank to finance her revolutionary activities. At first, I thought she was kidding. She later robbed a bank in Brighton. One of her accomplices shot and killed a Boston police officer. Susan was placed on the FBI's ten most wanted list.

"And then there was Abbie Hoffman. I was proud of him. I think he was a psych major who graduated in 1959," Roger added.

I then brought up, "His Yippie movement was what radical activism was *really* about. He's been the best politically active hippy."

Roger chuckled, "I loved it when they ran a pig for president. They had a real sense of humor."

Allen said excitedly, "They did terrific work staging protests at the 1968 Democratic National Convention and got what they wanted from that fascist Daley, which was the violent retaliation by police, and of course, the Chicago Seven trials."

I replied, "Yeah, they made their mark on the world."

We all stood silent for a while, old times and old stories swirling through our minds.

_____

Appendix B: A Comedian in the Family

A description of my dad in Wikipedia:

"Jason [my dad] was well-liked among entertainers. This is illustrated by a newspaper story about his son's bar mitzvah: 'The boy's father is the current comedy star at the Latin Quarter in New York City. Many show business personalities attended the service, including Jackie Mason, Phil Foster, Norman Dean, Lew Black, Davey Starr, Jack Kahane, Corbett Monica, Gene Baylos, Marilyn Maxwell, Tony Drake, Laura Lane, Tina Robin and Bea Kalmus.'[48]"

"From the 1950s to the late 1990s, Jason was one of the most enduring and recognized performers at Catskill Mountains' resorts. He played frequently at the Granit, Concord, Kutsher's Hotel, the Nevele, The Laurels Hotel and Country Club, The Pines Resort, Raleigh, the Overlook, the Tamarack Lodge, Stevensville, the Windsor, and Grossinger's Catskill Resort Hotel. As mentioned by Grosswirth, 'Jay's name will be familiar to those of you who used to frequent what was commonly referred to as 'The Borscht Belt'".[9] In a *Newsday* magazine article in 1992, reporter Stuart Vincent mentioned that Jay "is the consummate Catskills comic... You've probably seen him if you've been to one of the Borscht Belt hotels in the Catskills with your temple, your church, your parents, your cousins. A funny man. A comic's comic. An entertainer for 60 years—impressionist, singer, even has a few dance steps in him...he's played the Las Vegas hotels and Manhattan night clubs, appeared on "The Ed Sullivan Show" three times.'[10] "

"Rudd is quoted in *Jazz and its discontents*,[42] saying that 'Comedians are like the jazz musicians of the Borscht Belt, ... then there's Ralph

Pope, Jay Jason, Lenny Rush, and Mickey Marvin...they're incredible. And they do improvise, within a set form. They work with a set number of variables—like a musician would with, say, twelve notes—and they shift the order of things according to how the audience is reacting. They usually start out the same and have a big thing they do at the end that brings it to a peak and lets then bow out gracefully. Like a final coda or cadenza. But in the middle, you never know where they're going next. That's the exciting part'".

Publicity about my dad

Appendix C: Genealogy

The Starting Point is the Family

My dad's mother, Lina Wicks, had two sisters and five brothers. One by one, the family members left a little town near Galicia, Hungary, where they had a saloon, and moved to Rochester, New York in the early 1900s. My dad's father, Ben Levy, was born near the Black Sea in Russia. Around age nineteen, because of the ongoing pogroms, he came to America with his parents, two brothers, and three sisters. They also settled in Rochester toward the beginning of the 1900s.

My dad's grandmother named Sara had a father who was a rabbi. My dad was very close to his father's father, Abraham Levy, who was a learned man. My dad's grandfather studied the Torah and spent much of his free time in the synagogue. In the U.S., he worked as a cantor part-time, and during the daytime was a shochet, a person who kills chickens and other animals so that they are kosher. My dad spent Friday and Saturday nights with his grandfather, leading the life of an orthodox Jew. Because my dad's parents lived close to a cheder, a Hebrew school, my father sometimes lived with his grandparents. My dad loved his grandfather's big, warm voice, and hoped to one day be able to sing like him. Watching his grandfather as a cantor, and his two uncles and father in their choir, instilled the idea of entertaining other people. Although his grandfather was bright, he had a terrible temper, and verbal fights occurred frequently over small issues (e.g., his wife being late with the food). His grandfather was a significant role model for my dad. By living with his grandparents for extended periods, he assimilated tremendous respect for learning and Jewish tradition, and also the tendency to vent his anger toward family members when he was frustrated.

EXPERIENCING SACREDNESS: A PSYCHO-SPIRITUAL JOURNEY

My dad's parents, Lina and Ben, ran several businesses to support their family of six children. At different times his parents owned a grocery store, a hardware store, and a restaurant. During the depression, my dad's mother bought and sold houses. Lina had excellent business skills, and she ended up supporting the family. Her husband spent considerable time on the road as a shoe salesman, but he was never particularly successful. After my dad was earning high wages in show business, my dad often had to give his father enough money to buy supplies, and his dad could appear as if he was making money. Lina often lost her patience with Ben, and sometimes would yell at him. My dad identified with Lina, who was a bright, independent, and powerful woman. In later life, when my dad became angry, he adopted his mother's style of venting her anger; he would shout and be verbally abusive.

My mother's mother was named Ciel, and her mother was a Comer, a distinguished family that had been part of the Romanian aristocracy. My mother's grandparents did not work for a living, as they were associated with the royal court in Europe. When my mother's grandmother moved to this country, she divorced her playboy husband and became a businesswoman. She made fancy clothes and was self-supporting. She next married Mr. Weinberg, an engineer who spoke 18 languages and had previously constructed many bridges in Europe. When he came to this country, his degrees were not accepted, and he turned to be a healer, giving hot baths to people. My mother's mom, Ciel, had always been interested in occult practices (telling fortunes, reading tarot cards, etc.). As a youth, Ciel was very unhappy, and she repeatedly ran away from their home because her mother had a terrible temper. Ciel had been training to be an opera singer, but to escape oppressive home conditions, she eloped with Jack Peltz and gave up her career. My mother identified with her successful grandmother and aspired to be a successful businesswoman. She did not want marriage to limit her career as it had her mother's.

Jack Peltz, my mother's father, was from a large family, that emigrated from Russia. Jack's father was a butcher with 8 children. But he was an alcoholic and had a terrible temper. The Peltz family were fast, glib, and charming people; they could make mincemeat out of anyone. Jack became an alcoholic like his father, but he was also a financial wizard. Jack's first business was selling cigars. He next owned the first supermarket that was open for 24 hours in Cleveland. He also owned beauty shops. His greatest success occurred in the automobile business, where he owned the largest Ford auto distributor in Cleveland. Jack was the only Jew that Henry Ford hired to work in Detroit. Her father did more car business than anyone in Cleveland during the 1920s and 1930s. His genius was in knowing how to mount successful campaigns to sell automobiles, and he traveled throughout the U.S. training personnel in car dealerships on his techniques. My mother and her brother grew up in a family with wealth but incredible instability, as her father was constantly drinking. Jack made many fortunes but would spend most of his money on alcohol and girlfriends. His wife left him several times, but he would always pursue her and promise to repent. My mother would watch her father put together business deals, and she watched him destroy the businesses. My mother idealized her father for his brilliant mind, and she believed that she also had the talent to be successful in business. Knowing about my grandfather's alcohol addiction made me very cautious about drinking, and I stayed away from any illicit drugs, except for the one occasion in India when I did smoke marihuana that I had picked in the mountains.

Appendix D: Mythology

Transformational Theory

I read widely including the works of Joseph Campbell, Jean Huston, Carl Jung, Sigmund Freud, R.D. Laing, Alfred Adler, Viktor Frankl, and Albert Camus. Reading the work of intelligent and articulate scholars was helpful and continues to be so. We stand on the shoulders of those who came before us.

According to Jean Houston, myths help map our routes toward a deeper life, to the realm of amplified possibilities. Cultures once provided people with symbologies that refreshed the spiritual dimension. I had been seeking to find and articulate the myths I live by, the powers within myself that were asking for fulfillment and realization. During my trip to India, I realized that I must create personal answers to the metaphoric themes of what I might become. Recognizing the dark side within others and myself, forgiving those who manifested it, and not allowing it to dominate my life would provide me the opportunity to better appreciate spirituality.

Jung believed we have a collective unconscious, where forms or images from different cultures and historical periods appear. Within the collective unconscious are archetypes, like a hero who can overcome dragons and monsters. These hero images appear in each generation and allow ordinary people to free themselves from their misery and raise themselves to almost superhuman status and more complete fulfillment of their potential.

At the beginning stage of the mythical journey, I was developing myself and slowly becoming initiated into the adult world. Traditions, myths, and other guideposts helped me find who I was and integrate the shadows into my conscious life. The shadows are aspects of our existence that have been repressed, and for me, this involved my relationship with my charismatic dad. Freud and Bradshaw showed how children's experiences can be marred by parents' unrealistic expectations, abuse, and neglect. Karen Horney has also shown us the consequences of the absence of love, affection, and reliable care in childhood.

The Shadow

Adler has shown how early feelings of inferiority can predispose us to later strivings to reach unrealistic goals, and I was prone to this. These early experiences can cause emotional trauma in the child, and their effects can last through adulthood and continually sabotage our efforts to mend. My mythical journey included seeing these wounds and learning to interpret past events in ways that preserved my honor and integrity.

The next domain of the shadow involves the existential dilemma of living a life in which my social and biological needs are met, but in which my persona, the mask I wore, draws farther and farther away from my soul. Society often creates and requires that we wear a mask of respect and order. But according to Jung, severe problems can occur if the ego identifies with the mask. As R.D. Laing has suggested, this divided self will produce a vulnerability that can have devastating consequences.

It was clear to me that many people dislike their jobs and social roles, yet maintain their masks because they fear a future without the certainty of their lives. Taking off the mask marks the embarkment on a mysterious and frightening personal journey. It takes courage and faith to begin a journey toward authenticity, to follow my inner truth, as opposed to what society dictates.

My summer voyage helped me recognize the unparalleled opportunities that could be available to me by becoming a psychologist. I would help others take off their masks, and in doing so, I was fortunate to find my mission in life.

Other shadows that can be confronted on the mythical journey have been described by Jung. These shadows involve imbalance and the consequences of excess. Extraverts are active in the outer world to prove themselves. Introverts are open to the impact of experiences and intimately feel warmth and love for the world. These two aspects of my personality were in me and others, and my need was to learn to balance power and erotic drives. If one domain dominates the other, problems can occur.

Emilie, my soul mate and teacher in Israel, opened my heart so I could experience the sacredness of warmth and love. She helped me find a way to love and make peace with early childhood trauma. Even then, excesses on the Introvert-Extrovert dimensions can create vulnerabilities that can, over time, weaken the constitutional energies of the psyche. The mythical journey was to bring me into contact with those dimensions of my personality that have been underdeveloped or neglected.

The Need for Integration

Jung writes that I and others have masculine and feminine qualities. In metaphorical terms, both domains need to be honored and appreciated.

The psychological myths revolve around the development of myself, the recovery from childhood abuse or neglect, the development of an authentic self, and the integration of complementary aspects of my personality. Once these stages have been successfully achieved during the first part of my life, a different set of myths becomes more salient. During the second part of my life, metaphysical journeys begin. My journey started as an exploration of religions and spiritual issues. But I also realized the need to work on healing from the mythical issues that involved my childhood.

Mystical Second Half of Life

These journeys during the second part of life can involve opening one's heart to another person in a sacred marriage. In mythology, when the god marries the goddess, each has found his or her other half. Marriage becomes the prime event in their lives; they give themselves, not to each other, but to the marriage. Another metaphysical outcome is the development of a special and loving relationship with God. For example, in the father-son atonement myth, the disciple envisions the father-God as having transcendent energy. Finally, some myths feature an experience of oneness with the universe, such as in Buddhism, and this was a core motivating factor in my journey to India. With this new experience, the hero gains a protective distance from the terror that exists in the world, and at the same time can experience compassion and joy. The wonder and awe of the universe have now spoken directly to the hero's soul and opened up a heightened appreciation of the mystery of life, which for me culminated in a healthy and nurturing sacred relationship with Emilie, my Finnish girlfriend.

Logotherapy and Posttraumatic growth

Finding a purpose and meaning helps provide a sturdier foundation for being able to appreciate with gratitude the gifts of life. One of the most influential writers was Viktor Frankl, a psychiatrist who saw the horrors of concentration camps in World War II. He developed what is called Logotherapy when he found those who had meaning in life had a better chance of surviving these death camps. You can tolerate any pain if you have a reason for it. Frankl told the story of an elderly man depressed and sad after losing his wife and companion of 40 years. Frankl helped the patient realize that because his wife died before him, she had been spared the suffering and grief she would have experienced had he died first. So, in a sense, his loss had a purpose. When the patient realized this, he shook Frankl's hand and walked out with a new way of feeling about the death of his wife.

Frankl also tells the story of an inmate at a concentration camp who had lost his wife, his kids, and all his friends, and saw the hate that the Nazis had for the inmates. He realized that if he hated the Nazis, he would be no different from them. He decided to love everyone, even those who had killed his family. This love enabled him to survive the worst conditions anyone could have endured. It is hard to imagine the ability to get beyond one's hate and anger in his situation.

In more recent times, some of these ideas have been incorporated into a field now called Posttraumatic growth (Tedeschi & Calhoun, 2004). After struggling to handle highly stressful circumstances, some individuals report a greater appreciation of life, more meaningful relationships with other people, a sense of increased strength, the identification of new and different possibilities for one's life, and spiritual and existential growth. This growth does not occur as a result of the trauma, but rather as a result of trying to make sense of the new reality that one has. This allows a person to be more resistant to being shattered and can increase a sense of meaning and growth.

LENNY JASON

Appendix E: The Roots of Violence

Digging Deeply

In Dec of 2019, I posted a YouTube video on the Roots of Violence, which is available at https://youtu.be/QFa4IgRve5c. In this video, I state that it seems like we see violence everywhere, whether it is mass shootings or terrorism. Where does this violence come from? It was a central question I tried to answer during my trip to India. In my YouTube video, I examined this question and probed into our distant past to try to uncover the roots of aggression. Ideas from this video are contained in my 1997 book titled: *Community building: Values for a sustainable future*, my 2013 book titled: *Principles of social change*, and a 2022 chapter I authored with Karl Conroy titled: *Transformative Ecology: A theoretical approach to social change*.

The question about where violence comes from I tried to answer during my journey to India, and my *Transformational Theory* addresses this question. Below, I describe this theory that defines four choice points that represent potential vulnerabilities and corresponding protective factors. Despite originating at different historical time points, these choice points are always present and can help us better understand the roots of violence and why power abuse occurs.

The First Choice Point: Aggressive versus Cooperative Instincts

Between 95-99% of human history was spent hunting and gathering (Lorenz, 1966), and during much of this time, aggressive and even violent behaviors were essential for our survival, and they remain a part of us to this day. There are times when violent, aggressive behavior is necessary, such as when authoritarian regimes threaten our freedom and safety, such as genocide. It is important to recognize that highly aggressive and competitive tendencies are within our genes, as it dates back to our animal ancestry. Let's look at chimpanzees, our closest animal relative.

Jane Goodall observed tribes of chimpanzees behaving fiercely, fighting for territory, and systematically killing members of other groups. These aggressive, biological tendencies are mirrored in our history of continuous warfare and struggle for power. But Goodall's work also shows that there were also vibrant inner qualities such as abundant energy, playfulness, and vitality in chimpanzees. These genetically shaped characteristics also reside within our species as evidenced by the cooperative cultural practices of small-band hunter-gatherer societies, which included food-sharing, collective child-rearing, and the pooling of resources to build communal living spaces (Narvaez, 2014).

We share our ancestors' aggressive and cooperative instincts. Transformational Theory suggests that if there are no or very few constraints on aggressive tendencies, then we are vulnerable to the types of innate violent qualities that have contributed to the power abuses that we see so commonly in our world. Within our genes, we have the potential for the expression of self-serving, abusive expressions of power as well as altruistic, joyous aspects of ourselves that can be used to create communities that are healthy and supportive.

The Second Choice Point: Separation from Nature

Our species, for hundreds of thousands of years, lived intimately connected to the natural environment and was infused with an appreciation for nature. But we evolved, learning to use fire, make tools, and develop language. Around 10,000 years ago, Homo sapiens domesticated animals and began farming. This revolution secured a steadier and more reliable food supply, which in turn provided resources that allowed and stimulated the development of cities and civilization. This had enormous benefits including cultural expansion and the invention of writing. Growing agricultural innovations provided us the wherewithal to control the forces of nature, and this led to another choice point: to either sanctify and appreciate our connection to animals and the land or to repudiate and sever this connection. One path fostered interconnectedness and ecological diversity, whereas the other path fostered dominance and control of a world seen as dangerous and in need of taming.

The critical choice point facing us today is a respectful balance with nature or a need to control and dominate the forces of nature; these distinct paths have been with us for centuries, but now the consequences of these choices are more acute for our species' survival.

The Third Choice Point: Our Place in the Universe

Although disease and war did shorten people's lives, Stein adds that in pre-industrial times, life transformations were honored and saturated with meaning. For centuries, religions and rituals have sustained and nurtured our species and provided us with an underlying sense of meaning. Our closer inspection of the natural world during the Renaissance in the fifteenth century helped usher in the scientific revolution.

The products and discoveries of this revolution have fueled advances in medicine, transportation, and energy that have provided enormous benefits to our species. But the scientific revolution might also have made us vulnerable, as these advances in our understanding of the physical world led to a new way of thinking about our relationship to the universe. With the earth no longer seen as the center of the universe, and with evolution chronicling our descent from a common ancestor with chimpanzees, a new vulnerability emerged which could question the merit and very worth of past rituals and guides that had provided meaning. As an example, existentialists later claimed that meaning could only be found in the persistent struggle with the absurdity of life — such as in Camus's (1955) *The Myth of Sisyphus*.

From 1400 to 1800, most people were still connected to the land as farmers or tradespeople, and most continued to be members of one religion or another. But the vulnerability occurs if science erodes meaningful mythologies and customs that have helped us understand our place in the universe. Here is a choice point; the scientific revolution could help us appreciate and recognize our place in the universe, but these same discoveries could unwittingly strip us of our reasons for living and even undermine those social controls that moderate instinctual forces within us.

Science does not need to sterilize or diminish our place in the world. Jason (1997) stated that "On the spiritual path, the analytic, thinking mind needs to accompany and protect the open heart" (pp. 70). Abraham Maslow (1962) in *The Psychology of Science* offered an excellent example of this blending of intuitive and analytic ways of knowing. He contended that a Taoistic method of observation—one that does not interfere with or judge what it is observing—is better equipped to expand our understanding of the human condition.

The Fourth Choice Point: The Industrial Revolution

The final choice point involves urbanization and industrialization, which began in the early 1800s and was spurred on by advances in the scientific revolution. Slowly, there was less need for the vast majority of humans to toil on the land, as mechanization allowed for tremendous advances in food production and time for improvements in the quality of life. During this time, there was a movement of people away from rural, trade-based communities toward cities where social structures were markedly fluid and individualistic. As people moved to cities, for some, their former connections to a rich web of life that encompassed family and community may have begun to erode. In addition, urbanization and industrialization could have begun to replace the sense of coherence and satisfaction that many people had found in their work.

If maintaining contact with family and community is a requisite for wellness, a disturbing trend is that so many individuals feel isolated in environments where meaning is often focused on getting ahead, often at the expense of others. Today, this rupture of our connection with the land and community has been further exacerbated by the creation of an ever-intoxicating Internet world, which has exposed another vulnerability with the weakening of ties to family, friends, and community. Robert Waldinger's longitudinal study of adult development has found close relationships are better predictors of happy lives than social class, IQ, or genes (Caruso, 2016). I am not suggesting that the solution is to revert to an agrarian lifestyle, but rather to understand that we can reestablish intimate connections with others in urban dwellings that enhance our sense of community.

The Four Choice Points

It is important to consider the four choice points together. What occurred 10,000 years ago was that our species learned to cultivate the land and produce a more stable food supply, which paved the way for civilization. Humanity was presented a choice point in the wake of this revolution. We could assume a respectful approach toward the natural world or use our growing knowledge to control and dominate nature. Centuries later, the scientific revolution expanded our understanding of the universe as when Galileo invented the telescope to see the moon and recognize that we revolved around the sun. The scientific revolution presented our species with new understandings of the natural world, but a belief in only science might have begun stripping away the customs and beliefs of prior centuries. The industrial and computer revolutions, too, advanced our species' quality of life, but they also had the potential to separate us from closely-knit communities with ties to family and the land.

To the extent that humanity chooses to control the forces of nature, undermine cultural and religious belief systems, and sever ties with family, friends, and community, there is a potential for losing the protection of social and cultural support systems that have successfully regulated expressions of violence and aggression. It is important to also recognize that some ancient cultures, mythologies, and religions perpetuated human rights violations such as child abuse and the marginalization of women and that such practices should be condemned. Many of these practices are a product of the vulnerabilities we have discussed, but this is not a reason to lose sight of the many positive contributions that ancient traditions offer us.

The constant viewing of violence throughout the media and the Internet has led many to feel that there is more violence today. But according to Pinker (2011), evidence from multiple sources indicates that there is less violence and homicides over time. He credits this change to several factors including the rise of societies with central governments, particularly democracies. Feminization is another reason, as women have increased positions of power. There is evidence of less testosterone in our species over the past 200,000 years, which might have occurred through selective breeding of less aggressive people (like what has been shown with foxes bred for self-domestication, Trut, 1999). Finally, other factors Pinker notes are more logical thinking when making policies, and the mass media that allows us to perceive others as less dangerous.

While the percentage of deaths in the total population due to violent conflicts is at a historical low, the actual number of deaths has increased. Pinker has focused his work on rates rather than numbers, and even if these rates of physical violence are less, other forms of violence need to be considered including mass incarcerations, inequality, poverty, and racism. Climate change and the extermination of many animal species are not just innocent and unintended consequences of a growing world population and economic expansion. If violence is defined as physical force intended to hurt or kill someone, our planet has certainly been severely injured by our actions.

The Transformational perspective helps provide a deeper understanding of the breakdown of community values and the rise of power abuse that occurs in our society by reflecting on the past. Cooperation and altruism are enhanced when our species lives in balance with nature, when we embrace customs, beliefs, and value systems that affirm life, and when we are connected to family and community. In Jason (2013), I asserted that without this roadmap, "social activists may fail to navigate through seemingly intractable problems and [...] abuses of power" (pp. 158).

Other interventions have changed the social context along with other regulatory factors. Gary Slutkin, the founder of Cure Violence, deploys credible outreach workers to interrupt conflicts, treat the highest-risk individuals, and change community norms. This program has found 34-56% reductions in shootings and killings in sections of Baltimore (Webster, Whitehill, Vernick, & Parker, 2012), and is now being implemented in countries worldwide. At the policy level, when

Australia banned rapid-fire guns after a 1996 mass shooting, killings decreased. While there were 13 mass shootings before the gun law reforms from 1979 to 1996, there were no fatal mass shootings after the gun law reforms from 1997 to 2016.

These types of interventions do suggest that violence can be interrupted, but the transformational theory digs deeper, just like an archeologist, in trying to understand the customs, norms, and values of individuals within contexts that have been influenced by different historical eras. My thesis is that breakdowns of social and regulatory mechanisms, along with educational and economic inequalities have contributed to many of the symptoms of violence that we continue to witness. Interventions that promoted social justice are better understood and actualized when examining whether we are trying to live in balance with or trying to inappropriately control nature, whether we see scientific advancements in knowledge as bringing meaning or invalidating our sense of coherence, and whether our social settings promote social isolation or a richer sense of community.

Many feel that as each community is different, contextualism would suggest there are no laws or regularities common to all settings. I believe there are fundamental historical challenges that promote vulnerabilities or resilience. In some ways, the four choice points are a critique of the contextualist approach, and my position is that there are universal themes that should be considered in every context.

I have suggested that we need to consider a historical perspective as we conceptualize solutions to social problems. Social change agents who hope to create meaningful, lasting change require a theory that suggests deeper ways to combat social problems, address power abuse, and optimize wellness and a sense of community.

EXPERIENCING SACREDNESS: A PSYCHO-SPIRITUAL JOURNEY

A New Perspective

In my work toward social justice, I have come to realize that both psychological strategies strengthen inner resources through instilling hope, confidence, enthusiasm, and the will to live, including settings or communities to live in that are protected and nourishing. During my trip in the summer of 1971, I learned about these types of settings. But without road maps or guides, it might be difficult to design interventions that address the structural issues that are predisposing so many citizens to a sense of numbness, isolation, and alienation.

As indicated earlier, before the industrial age, there were rituals, customs, and rites that helped ease the transition from the dependent status of youth to the more independent role of adulthood. Past myths provided us with a more tangible sense of meaning by providing a comprehensive road map to imaginatively transform life's customs and routine. What I learned from my travels is that there are psychological and metaphysical themes, and their resolution greatly influences my sense of fulfillment and happiness. I needed to learn how to honor my thoughts, return to a balance with nature, and restore and honor symbols and traditions that have provided meaning to our lives—to restore a sense of connectedness with life that people once had with their communities and their land.

I now know that the task of a transformational change agent is to help each people and community find their personal and communal mythologies. People and communities can search for their own and other cultures, for those symbols and traditions that energize and vitalize them to provide a sturdy road map for this journey toward individual transformation and community change. Our work can support interconnectedness with the natural world and help us live in balance with nature, as opposed to trying to control her. Scientific and technological investigations are needed to help explore the mysteries of life, and reaffirm and validate the importance of rituals, traditions, and initiatory processes that help people and their communities mature and develop intimate bonds. We can attempt to recapture the sense of community that provides responsibility, mission, and commitment to the welfare of one's community.

My summer journey provided a foundation for this new perspective on life. I now see miracles happening if I'm willing to see them. I also know a subtle veil separates me from seeing the world either as a dark coal mine or a brilliant golden wonder. I realized there's always danger in the world, but even the worst experience has a redeeming part. You see, when we get unfairly criticized or attacked, we can better recognize that we're all prone to be wounded by others at some point. So, by forgiving others, we learn to forgive ourselves. Coming so close to real danger helped me put things into a new perspective. These experiences continue to be my guides, providing me with new ways of being in the world. These lessons are always with me if I'm willing to see and hear them.

Every person is complex and has many aspects to their personality. I recognized over time that my dad was not going to change. I tried to get in touch with my feelings of compassion for him and his suffering, and the pain he had inflicted on others. The seeds of critical perfectionism and hostility had been passed on to me. I would try to find a way to not allow these aspects of myself to destroy me and would learn to forgive and transcend these human emotions.

Real change involves providing those with fewer resources and more opportunities, but it also involves a new way of thinking, and many of the experiences I had during my summer voyage were instrumental for my later work. In other words, true liberation needs to occur in both the external and internal world. Jason and Moritsugu (2003) emphasize that we do not want to support interventions that help those in power to further control and dominate other people and our fragile environment. My trip helped me understand there is fundamental knowledge grounded in a sense of vibrant interconnectedness, one that embraces the unity in which we are embedded. It is through foundational values that our transformation can also help lead to the transformation of others through compassion, love, and empathy based on the interdependence of all things.

Appendix F: Positive Psychology and Meditation

From Deficits to Strengths

The initial reason for my journey to India was a search for God. I had been raised in a social ethic that is wonderfully described in a passage from Ari Goldman's book *The Search for God at Harvard*: "...Judaism was focused on doing, what we call mitzvahs, good deeds which we were told made us better Jews. In this system, understanding the nature of God is not important. Doing mitzvahs is what matters. There are 613 mitzvahs in the Torah and thousands more added by the rabbis in the Talmud and the legal codes that followed. ...God is, of course, somewhere in this system of mitzvahs, but the practitioner is usually too busy to notice."

During my training in the field of clinical psychology in the 1990s, deficits and negative emotional states were the focus, and based on my early experience with Maslow and my trip to India, I was certain there were large unexplored areas in psychology. Over the past 25 years, positive psychology has emerged as a field that borrows from humanistic psychologists and focuses on human strengths (Seligman, 2002). For example, emotional intelligence has assumed great importance involving emotional self-regulation, optimism, and empathy (Goleman, 1995), and even gratefulness and forgiving are becoming part of this movement (Luskin, 2002).

Mindfulness Meditation

EXPERIENCING SACREDNESS: A PSYCHO-SPIRITUAL JOURNEY

One example of these more positive approaches is mindfulness meditation, which involves sitting still and focusing exclusively on one's breath, to hone one's attention and maximize the unmediated direct experience. Mindfulness meditation is the basis of stress reduction programs operationalized by Jon Kabat-Zinn (Kabat-Zinn et al., 1992) and Richard Davidson (Lutz et al., 2008). It is thought that the effects of meditation rely on the body's ability to switch to an alpha (resting) or theta brain-wave state, and during meditation, the brain's rhythm slows and endorphins are released. As meditation practice is stabilized, these parasympathetic responses may be habituated and translated to daily life (Hsieh et al., 2007). Meditation has been found to increase blood flow to the frontal cortex, parietal and temporal lobes (Newberg et al., 2001), increase glucose metabolism (Herzog et al., 1990), and improve global functioning (Lutz et al., 2008). Meditation has also been demonstrated to cause neural reorganization and re-regulation in both novices and long-term practitioners (Lutz et al. 2008). Meditation practice might also be associated with changes in the brain's physical structure, as long-term meditation practice is associated with altered resting electroencephalogram patterns and is suggestive of long-lasting changes in brain activity (Goleman, & Davidson, 2017). These studies on the neurochemical effects of meditation on brain neurotransmitters, coupled with the established research on the neuroelectric effects of meditation, indicate several wide-ranging neurophysiological benefits of the regular practice of meditation.

This concept of mindfulness includes awareness, connection, insight, and purpose. Mindfulness also includes behavioral expressions of these concepts of mindfulness, including non-reactivity, which is directly related to the moderation of limbic activity. For those readers with an interest in reading more on this topic, the Mindfulness Adherence Questionnaire (MAQ) is a 12-item scale used to measure the amount (frequency, duration) and quality (attention, attitude) of formal and informal mindfulness practice engaged in by a respondent over the past week (Wong et al., 2016; Hassed et al., 2020). Also, the *Mindful Attention Awareness Scale (MAAS; Brown & Ryan, 2003)* is a widely used 15-item measure of present-moment awareness. The MAAS is responsive to mindfulness training, correlates in expected directions with measures of wellbeing, and differentiates between individuals with and without meditation experience (Brown & Ryan, 2003). Finally, the *Five Facet Mindfulness Questionnaire* (Baer et al., 2006) is a widely used measure designed to assess mindfulness across five dimensions: acting with awareness, observing, describing, nonreactivity, and nonjudging.

Below is an example of training for the Breath Counting Task (Moore, 2018): Sit in a meditation posture. Now breathing through the nostrils, bring your attention completely to that. The core of the method, now, is this: unite your mind with your exhalations by counting them. Whenever you inhale, just relax and remain present; that is, simply be aware of the whole-body sensation of inhaling. But when you exhale, count each exhalation mentally to yourself: "One..." And on the next exhalation, "Two..." And so on, until you have counted nine exhalations. When you reach nine, return to one and repeat the cycle.

But we need to also recognize that many individuals have limited opportunities living in impoverished environments and that we need to also direct our efforts at humanitarian efforts to bring about change.

Spiritual Awakening

From my journey, I learned that as individuals suspend their typical self-centered perspective, spiritual awakenings can occur suddenly or gradually, and are experienced as transcendence, a sense of connectedness, by feelings of oneness, or unity with something greater than oneself (McClintock et al., 2016), and is often accompanied by great knowledge or insight of one's true nature, purpose, or values (Cornielle & Luke, 2021). Sacredness often associated with experience includes a sense of bliss, gratitude, tranquility, and insight that love is the supreme principle in one's life (Taylor, 2017). Spiritual awakenings can also have profound positive effects on people in recovery (Bell, Islam, Bobak, Ferrari, & Jason, 2022).

Afterword

Reflections on the Journey

Nicole Porter

Reading through this travel journey evoked many recollections of how Dr. Jason has walked the meaningful walk throughout his impressive and distinguished career. *Experiencing Sacredness* is a beautiful compilation of events that portray the personal, challenging, evocative, revolutionary, pithy, erudite, and ongoing efforts of one person to discuss the universal necessity of the pursuit of finding meaning in life. This is an energizing vision, not only for the field of psychology but for every human being. Similarly, Dr. Jason outlines the evolving contours of a spiritual journey whose realization is constantly underway, not only in his personal life but also as universal truths expressed in the fields of post-traumatic growth, community, health, and positive psychology. The chapters outline the many ways in which Dr. Jason has sought to integrate social values and advocate a commitment to personal growth, with a rich and multi-layered conception of our world and our place in it.

Dr. Jason is on a mission, a calling, to create a rich identity for himself, those around him, and the field of psychology. His career, research, and mentoring style have served as an antidote not only to addressing the Jungian Shadow but also too much more; it has been one person's effort to reshape how we think about our academics, our interconnectedness with one another, and the meaning in our individual lives. The hallmarks of Dr. Jason's persistent urgings are found throughout: the importance of balance; respectful and dedicated commitment to community and the diversity therein; the centrality of relationships and compassion in creating goodwill; living in balance with nature; the importance of addressing our ancestral and intergenerational trauma; and balancing intuitive and analytic processes. He achieves this by returning to and acknowledging four themes: controlling our aggressive impulses, encouraging us to commune with nature, acknowledging our deep spiritual cosmology, and moderating the influence of the isolation caused by the industrial and technological revolutions. Here we have the continuation of the evolution of a dynamic ecological perspective, the conceptual glue that connects the balance points so central to Dr. Jason's thinking: interdependence and equilibrium.

Four Choice Points for a Renewing Spirit

The following four axes, or "Choice Points," have merit not only in contributing knowledge but also in benefiting our collective spirit. These are more than topics. Dr. Jason is suggesting that if we can continue to engage these axis points, orienting frames of reference, we can enlarge our spirit while we continue to create our identity so that our intellectual activities continue to be interconnected with our emotional and spiritual commitment to the field of psychology, and our personal lives. In thinking about ways to generate personal development, not just for us as individuals but also for our collective work, he offers these four dynamic systems' themes:

1. Balance in Community: Increase understanding of systems theory and interconnectedness to moderate aggressive impulses and increase compassionate communal drives;
2. Balance in Nature: Increase our ability to balance our stewardship of nature with our ability to dominate, in an active effort to commune with her;
3. Balance in Intuition: Increasing ties to our internal spiritual cosmology will balance the external emphasis of our current

dominant mode of analytic, scientific, and cosmological nihilism;

4. Grounding in Concrete Reality: Decreasing our emphasis on industrial and technological solutions and experience will increase our connection to the present moment and improve our overall well-being.

Implementing each of these suggestions makes us less dependent on science and the profession of psychology as our only source of intellectual exchange or mental and emotional well-being. Focusing on these Choice Points may keep us intimately involved with those soul mates from other walks of life. These are folks who are engaged in direct, local efforts to increase intimacy and knowledge within complex nuclear dynamic systems, as well as in larger communities and social structures. These intimate relationships are at the core of the human experience, personal growth, and healing trauma. These connections and the perspectives they afford are also potential antidotes against too precious elitism and isolationism when doing community psychology, engaging in public policy, and in pursuing an authentic life.

"On the spiritual path, the analytic, thinking mind needs to accompany and protect the open heart."

Leonard A. Jason, *Community building: Values for a sustainable future*

This is a quote I love, and it is central to this conversation. It bares noting that it presupposes that the heart is already softly open to be accompanied and protected. This journey seems to suggest that too often in modern society it is the reverse, with the intellect directing and dragging along a vaguely compassionate and hardening heart. This may be the balance to which Dr. Jason is pointing.

There is another feature. By investing in our four axes presented here, I believe Dr. Jason continues to suggest that we increase the

EXPERIENCING SACREDNESS: A PSYCHO-SPIRITUAL JOURNEY

interdependencies between our spirit and our actions in the physical world. The dichotomy between intention and action is de-emphasized in modern life, put aside, and even evaporated. By continuing to engage with nature, intimate and diverse individuals, and communities as systems, we may expand our analytical knowledge of how to better understand the innate resources and latent constraints affecting our concepts about other individuals, nature, and ourselves. By experiencing persons from diverse walks of life and unique lifestyles, we are stretching our ability for compassion, as well as our concepts, methods, and intuition. By knowing and working with our past trauma, we are keeping ourselves alert to the spiritual constraints that are limiting opportunities for personal development. Equally important, we can learn more about how personal developmental processes can bring about positive changes in individuals and ourselves by confronting our shadow and the trauma that gives rise to the masks we wear.

By emphasizing a commitment to a spiritual journey as a source of intelligence, explanation, and action, we are creating the possibility that our work breaks free of the constraints of egocentrism and scientism. This is when life becomes a psycho-spiritual journey. This is how we can begin to experience the sacred.

Dr. Jason has demonstrated these principles and walked the meaningful walk. His integrity and commitment to these principles will help others confront their shadow selves. A testament to this is an army of loyal and dedicated interns and mentees who experienced Dr. Jason's power to foster the best versions of themselves.

While his academic stature is undisputed, if it is true that greatness is "often seen in the little things," I believe he has achieved it here as well. Like Dr. Jason, these four axes continue to provide mentoring, energy, and excitement. I hope they can continue to be resources for you as well.

References

Adler, A. (1973). *The practice and theory of individual psychology.* Totowa, NJ: Littlefield, Adams.

Anderson, S., & Hopkins, P. (1992). *The feminine face of god.* New York: Bantam.

Baer, R.A., Smith, G.T., Hopkins, J., Krietemeyer, J., & Toney, L. (2006). Using self-report assessment methods to explore facets of mindfulness. *Assessment,* 13, 27–45.

Bell, J. S., Islam, M., Bobak, T., Ferrari, J. R., & Jason, L. A. (2022, June 2). Spiritual awakening in 12-Step recovery: Impact among residential aftercare residents. *Spirituality in Clinical Practice.* Advance online publication.

Brown, K. & Ryan, R. (2003). The benefits of being present: Mindfulness and its role in psychological well-being. *Journal of Personality and Social Psychology,* 84(4), 822–848.

Campbell, J. (1949). *The hero with a thousand faces.* New York: Pantheon.

Campbell, J. (1969). *The world mythology series.* Available from Dolphin tapes, P.O. Box 71, Big Sur, CA. 93920.

Campbell, J. (1971). *Hermes, alchemy, and the voyage of Odysseus.* Available from Dolphin tapes, P.O. Box 71, Big Sur, CA. 93920.

Campbell, J. (1980) *Transformation of myth through time.* Volume II. Available from Dolphin tapes, P.O. Box 71, Big Sur, CA. 93920.

Campbell, J. (1990). *The flight of the wild gander.* New York: Harper Perennial.

Camus, A. (1955). *The myth of Sisyphus and other essays.* Tr. Justin O'Brien. New York: Knopf.

Caruso, C. (2016, Oct 19). Men with happier childhoods have stronger relationships in old age. Scientific American. Available at: https://www.scientificamerican.com/article/men-with-happier-childhoods-have-stronger-relationships-in-old-age/

Chapman, S., Alpers, P., & Jones, M. (2016). Association between gun law reforms and intentional firearm deaths in Australia, 1979-2013. *Journal of the American Medical Association, 316*(3), 291-299. doi:10.1001/jama.2016.8752

Corneille, J.S. & Luke, D. (2021). Spontaneous spiritual awakenings: Phenomenology, altered states, individual differences, and well-being. *Frontiers in Psychology, 12,* 720579. doi: 10.3389/fpsyg.2021.720579.

Darwin, C. A. (1936). *The origin of species.* New York: Modern Library. (Original work published 1859).

DiGangi, J.A., Jason, L.A., Mendoza, L., Miller, S.A., & Contreras, R. (2013). The relationship between wisdom and abstinence behaviors in women in recovery from substance abuse. *American Journal of Drug and Alcohol Abuse, 39*(1), 33-37.

DiGangi, J., Majer, J., Mendoza, L., Droege, J., Jason, L. A., & Contreras, R. (2014). What promotes wisdom in 12-step recovery? *Journal of Groups in Addiction & Recovery, 9,* 31–39.

Dollard, J. (1949). *Criteria for the life history, with analyses of six notable documents.* New York, NY: P. Smith.

Durkheim, E. (1947). *The elementary forms of the religious life: A study in religious sociology* (J. W. Swain, Trans.). Glencoe, IL: Free Press.

Frankl, V.E. (1983). Meaninglessness: A challenge to psychologists. In T. Millon (Ed.).*Theories of personality and psychopathology,*(Third Edition) (pp. 256-263). New York: Holt, Rinehart & Winston.

Freud, S. (1914). *On the history of the Psycho-Analytic movement.* In Standard Edition, vol. 14. London: Hogarth Press and the Institute of Psycho-Analysis.

Goleman, D. (1995). *Emotional intelligence.* New York, NY: Bantam.

Goleman, D., & Davidson, R. J. (2017). *Altered traits: Science reveals how meditation changes your mind, brain, and body.* Avery, New York, NY.

Goodall, J. (1986). *The chimpanzees of Gombe: Patterns of behavior.* Boston: Bellknap Press.

Hsieh, C., Liou, C., Hsieh, C., Yang, P., Wang, C., Ho, L., & Chen, L. (2007). Noninvasive functional source imaging of the brain and heart. *The International Conference on Functional Biomedical Imaging,* 12, 245 – 246.

Ibsen, H. (1955). *Peer Gynt.* New York: Limited Editions Club.

Jason, L.A. (1997*). Community building: Values for a sustainable future.* Westport, CT: Praeger.

Jason, L.A. (2013). *Principles of social change.* New York: Oxford University Press.

Jason, L.A. (2019, Dec. 31). *Roots of violence.* YouTube video available at:

https://youtu.be/QFa4IgRve5c

Jason, LA. (2019). *Community Psychology*. Available at: https://academicminute.org/2019/04/leonard-jason-depaul-university-community-psychology/

Jason, L.A., & Conroy, K. (2022). Transformative Ecology: A theoretical approach to social change. In R. L. Miller (Ed.), *The Routledge research encyclopedia of psychology in the real world*. New York, NY: Routledge.

Jason, L.A., Glantsman, O., O'Brien, J., & Ramian, K. (Eds) (2019). *Introduction to the field of Community Psychology: Becoming an agent of change*. Rebus Press.

Jason, L.A., Helgerson, J.L., Torres-Harding, S., Fries, M., Carrico, A., & Chimata, R. (2004). A scale to measure wisdom: Socio-demographic and psychological characteristics. *The Humanistic Psychologist, 32*, 284-306.

Jason, L.A., & Moritsugu, J. (2003). The role of religion and spirituality in community building. In K. H. Dockett, G.R. Dudley-Grant, & C.P. Bankart (Eds.). *Psychology and Buddhism: From individual to global community*. (pp. 197-214). New York: Kluwer Academic/Plenum.

Jason, L.A., & Perdoux, M. (2004). *Havens: True stories of community healing*. Westport, CT: Praeger Publishers.

Jason, L.A., Reichler, A., King, C., Madsen, D., Camacho, J., & Marchese, W. (2001). The measurement of wisdom: A preliminary effort. *Journal of Community Psychology, 29*, 585-598.

Jason, J. (2021). Jay Jason. Wikipedia. Available at: https://en.wikipedia.org/wiki/Jay_Jason

Jason, J. (2021). Jay Jason. YouTube. Available at: https://www.youtube.com/user/JayJasonTribute

Joyce, J. (1986). *Ulysses*. New York. Vintage Books.

Jung, C. (1964). *Man and his symbols*. Garden City, NY: Doubleday.

Kabat-Zinn, J., Massion, A. O., Kristeller, J., Peterson, L. G., Fletcher, K. E., Pbert, L., Lenderking, W. R., & Santorelli, S. F. (1992). Effectiveness of a meditation-based stress reduction program in the treatment of anxiety disorders. *American Journal of Psychiatry,* 149(7), 936-943.

Kelly, J. G. (1990). Changing contexts and the field of community psychology. *American Journal of Community Psychology*, 18, 769- 792.

Kingry-Westergaard, C., & Kelly, J.G. (1990). A contextualist epistemology for ecological research. In P. Tolan, C. Keys, F. Chertok, & L. Jason (Eds.) *Researching community psychology. Issues of theory and methods.* (pp.23-31). Washington, DC: American Psychological Association.

Laing, R.D. (1967). *The politics of experience*. New York: Pantheon.

Lorenz, K. (1966). *On aggression* (M. K. Wilson, trans.). Brace & World, Inc.

Luskin, F. (2002). *Forgive for good*. New York, NY: HarperCollins.

Lutz, A., Slagter, H.A., Dunne, J.D., & Davidson, R.J. (2008). Attention regulation and monitoring in meditation. *Trends in Cognitive Sciences,* 12(4), 163-169.

Mann, T. (1995). *The magic mountain: A novel*. (John E. Woods, Trans.). New York: Knopf.

Moore, M (2018). *The Rinzai Zen Way: a guide to practice.* Shambhala Press, Boulder.

Narvaez, D. (2014). *Neurobiology and the development of human morality: Evolution, culture, and wisdom.* Norton & Company.

Newberg, A., Alavi, A., Baime, M., Pourdehnad, M., Santanna, J., & D'Aquili, E. (2001). The measurement of regional cerebral blood flow during the complex cognitive task of meditation: a preliminary SPECT study. *Psychiatry Research, 106,* 113-122.

Maslow, A. (1962). *Toward a psychology of being.* Princeton, NJ: Van Nostrand.

Maugham, S. (1944). *The razor's edge.* New York: Doubleday.

McClintock, C. H., Lau, E., & Miller, L. (2016). Phenotypic dimensions of spirituality: Implications for mental health in China, India, and the United States. *Frontiers in Psychology, 7,* 1600.

Milgram, S. (1963). Behavioral study of obedience. *Journal of Abnormal and Social Psychology, 67,* 371-378.

Perry, C.L., Komro, K.A., Jones, R.M., Munson, K., Williams, C.L. & Jason, L.A. (2002). The measurement of wisdom and its relationship to adolescent substance use and problem behaviors. *Journal of Child & Adolescent Substance Abuse, 12,* 45-63.

Pinker, S. (2011). *The better angels of our nature: Why violence has declined. Viking Press.*

Pokorny, S.B., Adams, M., Jason, L.A., Patka, M., Cowman, S., & Topliff, A. (2009). Frequency and citations of published authors in two community psychology journals. *Journal of Community Psychology, 37*(2), 281-291.

Schwartz, T. (1995). *What really matters. Searching for wisdom in America*. New York: Bantam.

Seligman, M. (2002). *Authentic happiness: Using the new positive psychology to realize your potential for lasting fulfillment*. New York, NY: Simon and Schuster.

Spretnak, C. (1991). *States of grace*. New York: HarperCollins.

Stein, M.R. (1960). *The eclipse of community*. New York: Harper Torchbook.

Stewart, P. K., Roberts, M. C., & Roy, K. M. (2007). Scholarly productivity in Clinical Psychology PhD programs: A normative assessment of publication rates. *Clinical Psychology: Science and Practice*, 14, 157–171.

Taylor, S. (2017). *The leap: The psychology of spiritual awakening*. New World Library.

Tedeschi, R. G., & Calhoun, L. G. (2006). Time of change? The spiritual challenges of bereavement and loss. *OMEGA - Journal of Death and Dying, 53*(1), 105–116.

The Tao-Path is not the All-Tao. *The name is not the thing named*. Translated by Aleister Crowley (1918). Available at: https://terebess.hu/english/tao/crowley.html

Tolan, P., Keys, C., Chertok, F., & Jason, L. (Eds.) (1990). *Researching community psychology: Issues of theory and methods*. Washington, DC: American Psychological Association.

Trut, L. (1999). Early canid domestication: The farm-fox experiment. *American Scientist, 87* (2), 160.

Webster, D.W., Whitehill, J.M., Vernick, J.S., & Parker, E.M. (2012). *Evaluation of Baltimore's* Safe Streets *Program: Effects on attitudes, participants' experiences, and gun violence.* Johns Hopkins Center for the Prevention of Youth Violence, Johns Hopkins Bloomberg School of Public Health, Baltimore, MD.

Wong, W. P., Hassed, C., Chambers, R., & Coles, J. (2016). The effects of mindfulness on persons with mild cognitive impairment: Protocol for a mixed-methods longitudinal study. *Frontiers in Aging Neuroscience*, 8, 156.

About the Author

As a professor of psychology at DePaul University in Chicago and the director of the Center for Community Research, I have published articles on a range of social and health topics, from the prevention of, and recovery from, substance abuse; to preventive school-based interventions; to post-viral diseases, like long COVID, and Myalgic Encephalomyelitis/Chronic Fatigue Syndrome. I have written or edited over 30 books.

Some of my work at DePaul University has involved the creation of a Foundational Values Scale, a scale that measures the construct of wisdom, with ideas borrowed heavily from eastern religions (DiGangi, Jason, et al., 2013; DiGangi, Majer, Mendoza, Droege, Jason, & Contreras, 2014; Jason et al., 2001; Jason et al., 2004; Perry, Komro, Jones, Munson, Williams, & Jason, 2002). The first component, Harmony, consists of items assessing balance, self-love, good judgment, appreciation, and purpose in life. One is less burdened with stress to the extent to which one is balanced, has an appreciation of life, and can cope with uncertainty. The second component of the Foundational Values Scale, Warmth, includes kindness, compassion, and animation. The qualities of kindness and compassion are related to being in the present and having a sense of humor. This dimension includes the extension of hope and happiness to others through warmth, humor, and kindness. The third component of the scale is Intelligence. It appears that it is not merely the quality of intelligence but how it is used that determines its connection to wisdom. Using one's intelligence to solve problems and help others appears to be a key feature of wisdom-related intelligence. Nature is the fourth component, and it includes concern and reverence for the environment, and a sense that all life is interconnected. This concern for the environment is also related to the experience of flow, for it is perhaps one's love for and appreciation of the external world that allows one to be so deeply involved in an activity that nothing else matters. This dimension has been practiced by Native Americans for thousands of years, as they have revered and remained in balance with nature (Spretnak, 1991). The final component, Spirituality, consists of living a spiritual life and having a fellowship or union with God.

Ingram Content Group UK Ltd.
Milton Keynes UK
UKHW011954090423
419863UK00004B/544